Things to make with LEATHER

TECHNIQUES & PROJECTS

By the Editors of Sunset Books and Sunset Magazine

LANE BOOKS • MENLO PARK, CALIFORNIA

Foreword

The beauty and usefulness of leather have generated an appeal that has spanned centuries. Those who enjoy working with their hands will find making things out of leather highly rewarding. In this book, the basic leatherworking materials, tools, and techniques are described. In addition, a major section focuses on specific leathercraft projects and detailed instructions for making them.

Many people have helped with the book through their advice and through contributing examples of their leatherwork. We thank Brian Burns, Mary Louise Carter, Sylvia Grainger, The Leather Works of Palo Alto, Steve Smith, Gay Stafford, William J. Shelley, and Randi Vreeland.

Edited by Richard Osborne

Design by John Flack

Illustrations by Penelope Graham

Front Cover: Photograph by Ells Marugg.
Purse and sandals by Mary Louise Carter.

Photography by Lars Speyer, except for Alyson Smith Gonsalves: pages 12-15 (left), 16 (left), 17 (right), 18 (right), 19; Richard Osborne: page 41; Norman A. Plate: page 73; William J. Shelley: pages 76 (right), 77-80; Darrow M. Watt: pages 25, 35, 36, 54, 55, 58, 77 (bottom).

Executive Editor, Sunset Books: David E. Clark

Second Printing May 1973

 Library of Congress No. 72-92511. Title No. 376-04461-6. Lithographed in the United States.

Contents

THE *NATURAL* APPEAL OF LEATHER

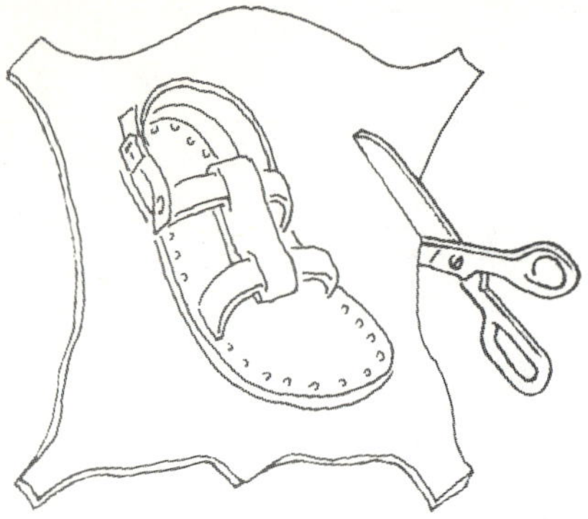

Who can resist touching things made of leather? Every characteristic of leather—its warm colors, rich texture, and clean, natural aroma—provokes luxurious and sensuous feelings.

The greatest appeal of working with leather is certainly the beauty of the material itself, but this is not the only attraction.

Leather is an extremely versatile and durable material that can be used on a large or small scale—for furniture upholstery, luggage, clothing, or shoes, or for accessories such as belts, wallets, and purses.

Its rare combination of beauty and function gives leather an appeal amounting almost to a mystique. And creating with leather satisfies both your esthetic and practical instincts, allowing you to make handsome articles that will last for years, often improving in appearance with age.

An Approach to Leathercraft

Working with leather is a freewheeling craft that can be approached in a number of ways: as a dabbler's brief stopover, as an artist's experiment with a new media, or as a master-craftsman's way of life.

If you are new to leatherwork and only want to make one or two things, you will be pleasantly surprised to learn that you can begin such projects as a wallet (pages 45-47), a purse (pages 48-51), or a belt (pages 36-40) without a large investment in tools and materials and without long sessions of preliminary practice.

Advanced leathercraft, though, can involve a high degree of skill and creative design, as in the suitcase (pages 56 and 57) and sandal making (pages 60-65). Many craftsmen develop their work into a fine art.

Leathercraft will also accommodate a less traditional outlook. Some people who prefer a casual approach find leather a rewarding media for self-expression. The leather mobile (page 80) and sculptured form (page 79) are some of the ways contemporary craftsmen and artists have expressed themselves in leather.

Whatever your approach to leathercraft may be, you'll find a project or idea to suit you on pages 34-80.

If you are an experienced leathercraftsman, you'll probably want to turn directly to the projects and begin working. But if you are new to leatherworking, it would be a good idea to skim through the first three chapters on leather, tools, and techniques. Then, after choosing something that you'd like to make and reading the instructions carefully, return to the chapters to pick up details and terms you may have missed the first time.

Looking Back at Leather

The fact that the Roman legions of Caesar's time moved across the seas on ships with leather sails gives some idea of how long leather has been of use to mankind. But leather's history goes back far beyond the period of the Roman Empire.

Leather's origins are rooted in prehistoric man's first use of untreated wild animal skins as clothing. Probably the skins were worn in the belief that the strength and ferocity of an animal were transferred to humans who wore his skin. Skins were also worn by hunters to disguise them from their prey.

As methods for preserving raw animal skins developed, leather as we know it began. Bas-reliefs from ancient Egypt, dating back to 4000 B. C. depict leathermakers at work. The carvings show that leather processing (probably with vegetable juices) had been known about at a very early date.

One of the oldest known "tanning" or preserving formulas for leather comes from ancient Babylonia, where raw animal skins were treated in allum, gallnuts, myrrh, oil, and sumac to make them durable.

Early leather was undoubtedly crude and took a long time to make, but it was still a very much used material.

Though we would never imagine modern America Cup yachts having leather sails, the Vikings and ancient Romans equipped their war ships with them, probably because leather was the strongest material available for the job. The strength and durability of leather were also probably the reasons that the Sumerians, in 3000 B. C., made tires for their chariots out of leather. Other peoples, including the American Indian, Australian aborigine, and primitive tribes of Africa and South America, also found that the toughness of leather made it suitable for shields, armor, and shelter.

Leather storage vessels of all types—for grain, wine, water, tools, and household utensils—have been found in archeological excavations in Greece, Egypt, Britain, and the Near East. In some cases, they date back to Neolithic times.

LEATHER SHADOW PUPPETS from Indonesia cast dramatic outlines; movable arms are connected with wire.

Interesting, too, are the leather shadow puppets, common in the Far East and South Sea Islands, which are perforated with tiny holes that produce a delicate, lacy shadow when a light is placed behind them to project their outlines onto a screen.

Mystical associations with leather are shown by the use of leather for religious fetish figures, notably by African tribes and the sinister voodoo cults in Cuba and Haiti.

By the time of the discovery of the Americas, leather was in widespread use throughout the world. In Europe, leather was being produced primarily by curing the skins in solutions made from the bark of various trees such as the oak, birch, and hemlock.

The first European settlers in America had brought leather with them. But shortly after becoming established, they built the first tannery in the New World in 1623.

As leather production in America grew, leather became widely used for everything from harnesses, saddles, clothing, and rope to window panes.

Leather was in such demand all over the world in the 19th century that in California, during the Spanish and Mexican periods, cowhides were one of the principal commercial exports and were even considered a form of money.

Leather Today

Smothered by an avalanche of mass-produced items made out of plastic and other synthetics, people today find that the natural beauty of leather (and especially hand-crafted leather articles) strikes the eye more than ever before.

The development of modern chemistry and manufacturing techniques has revolutionized leather production. In the 19th century, it took months of soaking hides in large pits filled with tanbark and other materials to make leather; now, a batch of hides can be processed within a week.

Fast, modern tanning methods are also highly controllable, enabling manufacturers to make leather with many desirable qualities from the same species of hide. This has broadened the uses of modern leather considerably.

Of course, we don't use leather for sails as the Vikings and Romans did, nor do we have leather tires on our automobiles. But the popularity of leather sandals (a footwear dating back to ancient Egypt), leather wallets, belts, purses, luggage, and clothing is attested to by the many leather shops, craft fairs, and boutiques selling leather goods. In addition, the craft of leatherworking is being spread more and more through classes both in public and private schools, in community adult education programs, and even in some leather shops.

CHOOSING HIDES AND SKINS

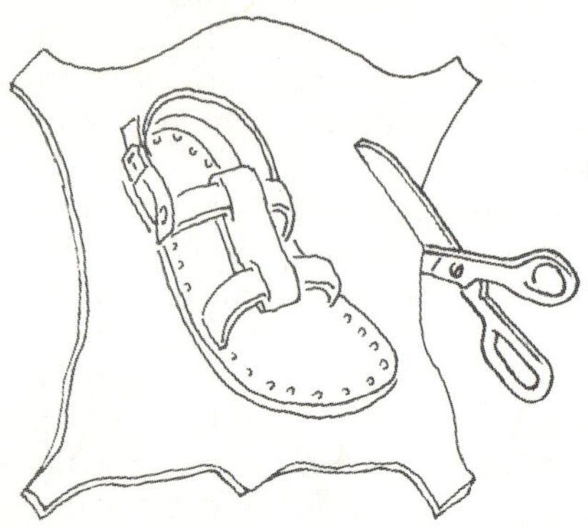

Of all the things you might learn about leather, probably the most central is that it is a *natural* material—a material that "breathes" and responds to care in much the same way as your own skin does. Many kinds and types of leather can be made, but they all share these characteristics.

Once you have developed a taste for leather, though, and a desire to make leather articles yourself, other facts will need to be gathered. You will probably be asking yourself at least three important questions: 1) How are animal skins processed into leather? 2) What different kinds of leather are available? 3) Where can I purchase leather and leathercraft supplies? On the following pages all of these questions are answered.

WHAT IS LEATHER?

Leather is simply the hide or skin of an animal treated in various ways to turn it into a workable, long-lasting material. The "hide" (or skin if the species is a small one) of practically any animal, including cattle, sheep, wild game, and reptiles can be used, each producing a different kind of leather with its own particular qualities and characteristics. All leather, however, is uniquely different from both woven fabrics, such as cotton, and continuous sheet materials, such as plastic.

Composed of innumerable small, randomly structured, and tightly interlocking fibers, leather is extremely strong and practically impossible to tear or puncture. The fibers also prevent its edges from fraying or unraveling. Not only is leather durable, but also the porous skin cells have a natural breathing ability that makes leather an excellent insulator and garment material.

HOW LEATHER IS MADE

Leather begins as the "pelt" of an animal which would harden and putrify unless specially treated. By soaking the pelt in certain chemical solutions (a process called "tanning") it can be preserved. Several tanning agents can be used: primarily chromium salts, vegetable products, and animal oils, each of which brings out different characteristics in the pelt and produces a different type of leather.

Only one of the agents can be used, or the leather can be treated in several of them through a process known as "retanning," in which the leather is tanned a second time to give it qualities of the other tanning agents. Though a pelt technically becomes leather after tanning, other processes both before and after tanning will give the leather qualities that tanning alone doesn't.

Before tanning, the manufacturer has an option of leaving the natural hair of the animal on the hide or removing it. Because the hair of full-grown cattle is thick and rather coarse, it is generally removed. The side of the leather that the hair was on is then called the "grain side"; it has a smooth surface, textured only by the natural skin cells and pores. The other side is known as the "flesh side" and has a coarser, rougher surface. The grain side is generally considered the more attractive side of leather, unless the flesh side has been sueded (page 8). Some animals, notably sheep and calves, have finer, more attractive hair that is sometimes left on the hide to produce specialty leathers.

The thickness of the leather is adjusted after tanning by large cutting machines that shave down the surface of the flesh side of the hide. A full range of thicknesses is possible, the only limit being the original thickness of the hide itself.

After thinning, the leather is sometimes retanned in tanning solutions not used in original tanning. Retanning is optional and most often done only to chrome-tanned leather to give it characteristics of vegetable- or oil-tanned leather. During the retanning (or sometimes the original tanning), the leather is dyed by mixing color pigment right in with the tanning solution.

At this point in leathermaking the hides are still wet from tanning solutions and rinsing. If hard, stiff leather is desired, the manufacturer can simply spread the hides out flat and allow them to dry. Softer leather, however, is produced by stretching and kneading the leather through large machines to loosen the fibers so that they can more easily bend and flex.

After drying, the final treatment is finishing. Leather is often left unfinished, especially if vegetable or oil tanned, but artificial finishes are sometimes applied (mainly to chrome-tanned leather) for special effects or protection.

Perhaps the best-known artificial finish is suede. Suede has nothing to do with the animal that the hide or skin came from. Rather, it is produced by lightly sanding or buffing the surfaces of the leather to produce a velvety nap.

Stamping patterns and textures onto the surfaces is another finishing process often used, especially on chrome-tanned leather. Frequently, embossed and stamped patterns are applied to make the leather look as though it were made from an exotic animal such as alligator or ostrich.

Protective finishes such as waterproofing and acrylic paints can also be applied to leather.

DIFFERENT KINDS OF LEATHER

Of the many different animals whose pelts can be made into leather, those commercially raised for meat are most commonly used since their hides are available to tanners in large quantities from slaughter houses. The kinds of leather you are most likely to find available are therefore cowhide, sheepskin, and calfskin. Other leathers you might see and want to try using are goatskin, pigskin, lambskin, deerskin, and horsehide.

Cowhide

If you go into a store and ask for leather, the salesperson will more than likely assume you just mean cowhide. Many types are available: thick, thin; hard, soft; finished, unfinished. And one kind or another can be used to make everything from belts and wallets to sandals and garments.

Various types of cowhide are generally referred to by the tanning method used to make them. With the exception of garment cowhide, however, all types can be used for the same sorts of projects, and distinctions between them needn't be a concern unless you are after special effects such as tooling, stamping, and dyeing.

Latigo. Cowhide tanned in animal oils is a good, all-around, versatile leather, generally known as "latigo." Because the animal oils tend to lubricate the leather fibers, latigo is somewhat flexible and has a soft surface and slightly oily feel. But latigo is still a good strong leather, available in a full range of thicknesses, and can be used for belts, purses, sandals, and many other articles.

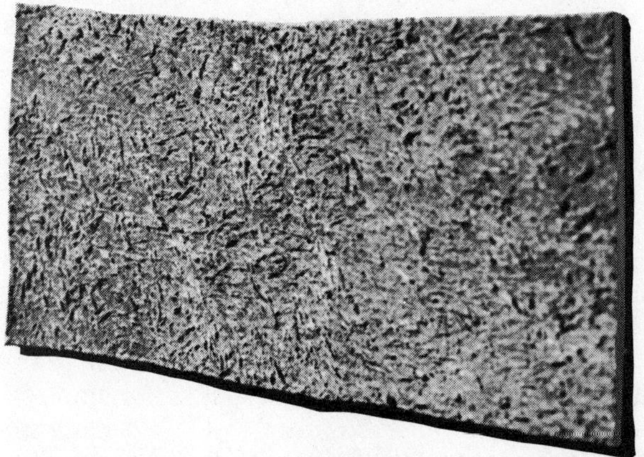

FLESH AND GRAIN (left and right) sides of cowhide leather have a smooth and coarse texture respectively.

SOFT, SUPPLE, and relatively thin, this piece of top grain cowhide has been sueded on only the flesh side.

EMBOSSED GRAIN patterns on samples of chrome-tanned cowhide are examples of artificial finishes applied to leather.

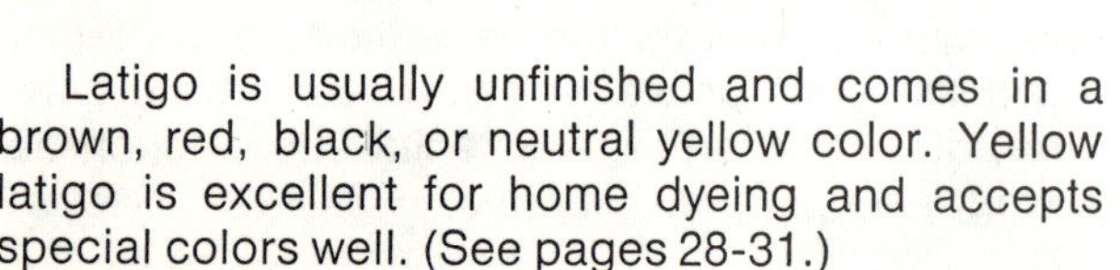

Latigo is usually unfinished and comes in a brown, red, black, or neutral yellow color. Yellow latigo is excellent for home dyeing and accepts special colors well. (See pages 28-31.)

Vegetable-tanned cowhide. Among the oldest tanning agents known are the tannin acids in certain plants, primarily the bark of various species of oak trees. "Bark" or "oak" tanned cowhide is drier and stiffer than latigo and has a harder surface; some craftsmen feel this surface makes oak-tanned leather best for tooling and stamping. Oak-tanned cowhide also is usually used for the bottom soles of sandals and other items requiring maximum strength. Otherwise, oak-tanned cowhide has the same all-around versatility as latigo and comes in the same wide range of thicknesses. Oak-tanned leather is usually unfinished and has a buff tan color that can be home dyed or left natural. (See pages 28-31.)

Chrome-tanned cowhide. Today, practically all leather is chrome tanned. Various chromium salts are the primary agents, but the leather is frequently retanned in oil or bark to give it qualities of oak tanning and latigo.

Because chromium salts leave the hides a bluish color, the leather is usually dyed at the tannery during or right after the tanning process. In feel and body, chrome-tanned cowhide is more like latigo; softer and a bit more flexible than oak-tanned leather. It is often stamped or embossed or given an acrylic finish. Chrome-tanned leather is rather difficult to home dye.

Garment cowhide. Generally chrome tanned and sueded, cowhide leather suitable for use in making garments is thin and supple. Several layers of garment weight leather can often be sliced from a single hide. Layers taken from the flesh side of the hide are called "splits" and are usually sueded on both sides. The topmost layer, having the smooth grain side on top, is called "top grain" leather; it is sueded on only the flesh side.

For maximum flexibility, garment leather is stretched and kneaded through large rollers to loosen the fibers. Depending on where you shop, a full range of tannery colors may be available. Since home dyes usually mat down or stiffen the nap of suede, you shouldn't try to dye suedes yourself.

Other Kinds of Leather

Calfskin, sheepskin, goatskin, deerskin, and pigskin don't have the same wide range of uses of

SOFT AND WOOLLY, this sheepskin was tanned with the natural hair still on the skin. The flesh side was sueded.

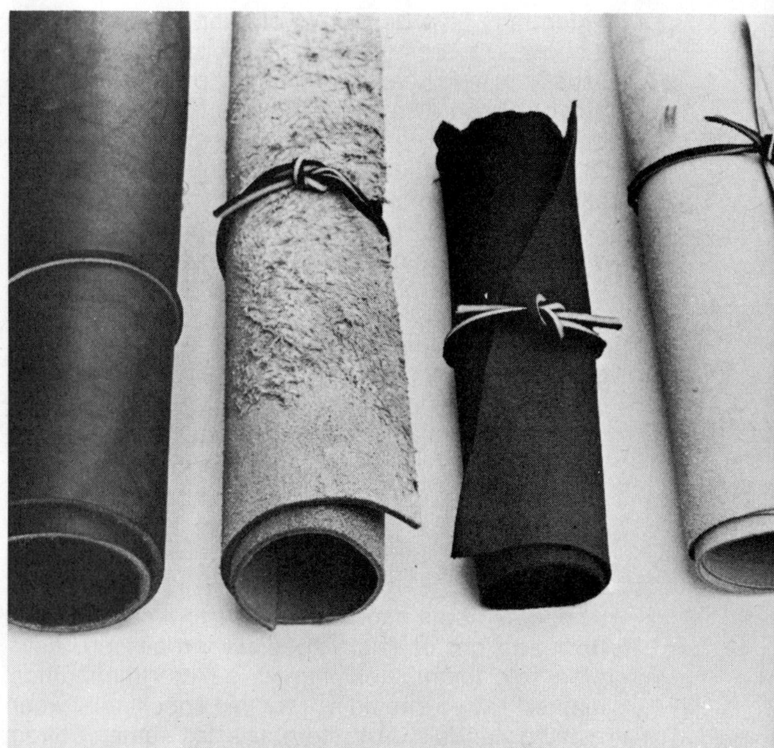

COMMONLY USED leather thicknesses are, from left to right: 8 ounces, 6 ounces, 4 ounces, and 1 ounce.

cowhide leather, but they are attractive and, if available, you might want to try using them.

Exotic types of leather, such as reptile and wild game skins, may require a search to find. Don't be fooled if you do see leather called "alligator," "sea turtle," or "ostrich"; cowhide is sometimes given an artificial grain pattern or texture resembling an exotic animal and then named after it.

Calfskin. The skin of young cattle produces a leather that is finer and more smoothly textured than leather made from more mature cattle. Usually oak or chrome tanned, calfskin is generally thinner than cowhide and used for small items such as wallets, billfolds, and linings.

With the natural hair of the calf still on, calfskin leather is attractive for trim and novelty items.

Sheepskin. Thin to medium weight, sheepskin is usually chrome or oak tanned for use as a garment leather and small articles.

Known as "woolskin," sheepskin tanned with the natural wool still on is very attractive for coats, pillows, and vests. Woolskin is usually sueded on the flesh side and the wool trimmed evenly to ¼ or ¾ inch long.

Goatskin, deerskin, pigskin. Thin, supple, and primarily used for garments, gloves, and small items, goatskin and deerskin have a unique "feel" and grain pattern.

Pigskin is a thin to medium-weight leather. Though hard to find, it makes nice handbags, garments, and small projects.

CHOOSING LEATHER

Rules prescribing certain kinds of leather for specific jobs don't really exist. In selecting leather, your personal taste and the project you want to make will be the primary guides.

With your project in mind, look at and feel different leathers. Do you want the finished project to maintain its shape or be soft and pliable? Will the article be subject to wear and tear? Do you want a heavy, sturdy appearance or a finer, more delicate one? Is the finished article going to be small or large?

A practical and easy guide for choosing any kind of leather is thickness, since more than anything else this determines bulk, flexibility, body, and strength. The tanning method may enter the picture to some extent, but it shouldn't be a major concern unless you are after special effects. Most leather is chrome tanned except for cowhide, which may also be oak or oil tanned. If you have a choice, just remember that oak-tanned leather is usually stiffer, harder, and drier to the touch than oil- or chrome-tanned leather. For this reason, many craftsmen prefer it for tooling and stamping. Otherwise, the different types can be used for basically the same sorts of things.

Thickness is measured according to the number of ounces one square foot of the leather weighs. By shaving down the flesh side of the hide, practically any thickness can be produced. Since cowhide is the thickest kind of hide to begin with, a full range is available from 3/16 inch (12 ounces) to 1/64 inch (1 ounce). Because other animals don't have as thick skin as cattle, not as wide a range of thicknesses can be made from their hides.

When looking at leather, remember that a piece usually appears thinner and more flexible on the sales counter than it will when made up into a project.

A note about sandal soles: bottom soles should be made out of thick, specially processed, cowhide sole leather (sometimes called "mechanical leather"). You should ask for this specifically when making sandals. An alternative to leather bottom soles is hard rubber (neoprene), which provides much better traction than leather. It is available at some leathercraft stores and at most shoe repair shops. The top soles of sandals are usually made from 5 to 8 ounce cowhide—oil or chrome tanned.

Following is a list of popular articles indicating the weights and kinds of leather frequently used to make them. The description of each project on pages 34-80 also includes the kinds of leathers to use. Don't feel that you have to follow the list and suggestions dogmatically. A difference of 1, 2, or even 3 ounces usually won't make very much difference in many projects.

Belts	8-9 ounce cowhide: latigo, oak, or chrome tanned for a 1 to 2-inch-wide belt; 4-6 ounce cowhide for thinner belts.
Billfolds	2-4 ounce cowhide, calfskin, pigskin or other leather.
Garments	1-2 ounce garment-type cowhide or any other soft, supple leather such as goatskin, pigskin, or deerskin.
Moccasins	4-5 ounce "moccasin" weight, sueded cowhide.
Purses	6-7 ounce leather for large purses; 4 ounce leather for small, lightweight purses.
Sandals	Top soles: 6-7 or 8-9 ounce cowhide, latigo or chrome tanned. Straps: 6-7 ounce latigo or chrome-tanned cowhide. Bottom soles: cowhide sole leather or hard-rubber soling material.
Wallets	2-4 ounce cowhide, calfskin, pigskin, or other thin leather.
Watchbands	2-4 ounce cowhide.

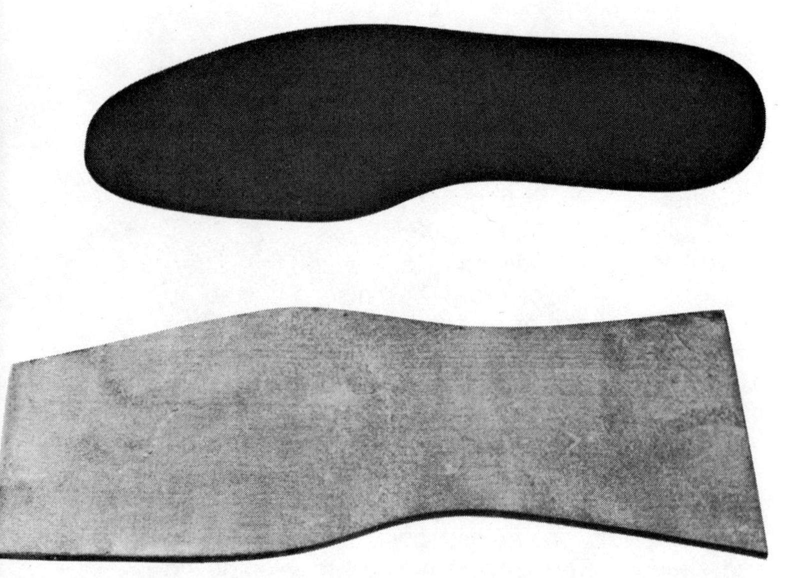

SANDAL SOLES can be made from two kinds of material: hard rubber (top) or cowhide "mechanical leather" (bottom).

WHERE TO FIND LEATHER

Tanneries and shops that sell leathercraft supplies and/or custom-made leather goods are the most likely sources for leather. Other places to look for leather are general craft supply stores and hobby shops. If they don't stock leather, ask if it can be ordered for you through a leathercraft mail order house. You should be able to find store listings in the yellow pages of the phone directory. If you have a problem finding leather, check shoe and luggage repair shops and saddlery stores. Even though they may not have leather in stock for retail sales, they might be willing to order what you want from their supplier.

Though many kinds of leather are produced, all types probably won't be available at the store you shop at. Most stores normally carry cowhide in several thicknesses along with garment leather and perhaps a selection of sheepskin and calfskin. Other kinds may or may not be stocked. If you want a leather that the store doesn't carry, ask if it can be specially ordered.

Buying Leather

Leather is priced by the square foot, but since hides and skins are oddly shaped, they can't be conveniently cut to the measurements you need as other fabrics can.

Shops usually purchase leather from tanneries by the whole hide or skin whose size depends on the species of animal the leather was made from. Cowhides are the largest—between 40 and 50 square feet. Tanneries usually cut hides in half, however, making two "sides" so that the leather will be easier to handle. Other common pieces are backs (7-10 square feet if taken from a side; 15-17 square feet if cut from a whole hide) and bellies, which are about 7 or 8 square feet. Backs are the least stretchy part of a hide and best for articles requiring strength, such as belts. Stretchy and irregularly shaped, bellies are considered the least desirable section but still can be used for many projects if you are not particular. Most other animal hides are smaller than those of cattle: sheepskin, 7-10 square feet; calfskin, 6-10 square feet; deerskin, 11-13 square feet.

Some shops will cut small pieces from a hide or skin on order; others will only cut a skin in half. But many shops won't cut hides and skins at all because this creates excess scrap.

If you only want to make one or two items and have no definite plans for future projects, try to shop at a store that will cut pieces to the size you need. You may have to pay extra for this custom cutting service, but you will avoid making a large investment in materials.

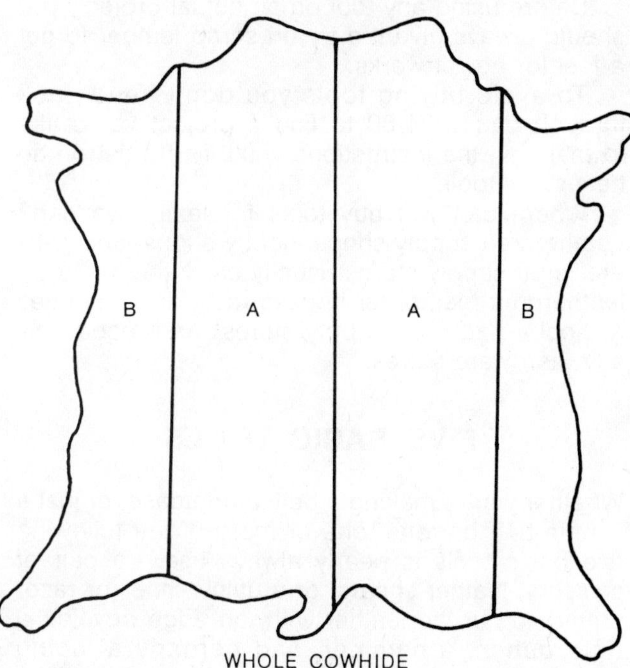

COWHIDES are often cut into small sections: side, A and B; back, one or both sections labeled A; belly, B.

If you expect to be making many articles from the same kind and weight of leather, the least expensive way of buying is in bulk—by the hide, side, or skin.

When purchasing any leather, spread it out on a table first and look for scratches, scars, holes, and brands. Leather is graded and priced according to its blemishes (or lack of them). Grade A is free of marks, scars, and holes, and the most expensive; grades B and C are blemished and therefore less expensive. Although you can cut around markings, doing so creates excess scrap.

Another thing to remember when purchasing leather in bulk is that the larger the hide or skin, the more likely it is that the animal was old and his skin stretchy and blemished.

Always take a pattern of your project shopping with you so that you can lay it out on the leather you want to buy. This will assure your getting the right amount of leather with as few scraps as possible.

Pre-cut straps, laces, and strips for belts (called "belt blanks") are generally standard items in leather shops. You won't have to cut them from a large piece of leather or have the leather shop custom cut them for you.

Another way of buying leather that you won't want to overlook is in bags by the pound. Shops usually sell or give away their scraps this way, and you'll find that many small and large items can be made from the pieces in these scrap bags. (See pages 78-80 for ideas about articles you can make with small pieces of leather and scraps.)

Reusing Old Leather

Never discount the idea of reusing old leather taken from leather articles that have broken or worn out. Shoes, belts, wallets, briefcases, purses, and luggage are all possible sources. Even if torn, badly scuffed, or discolored, old leather usually can be salvaged, renewed, and made into useful items.

Before starting to take apart something made out of leather, first make sure that the article is absolutely irreparable. Often merely a stylish buckle or a few more buckle holes in the end will restore a belt. Refinishing and dyeing, perhaps a new clasp or hinges, may be the only first aid that a purse or suitcase needs.

You'll be surprised at how much life can be restored to leather by just conditioning, refinishing, or a touchup dye job. (See pages 32-33 for conditioning leather.)

TOOLS YOU'LL NEED

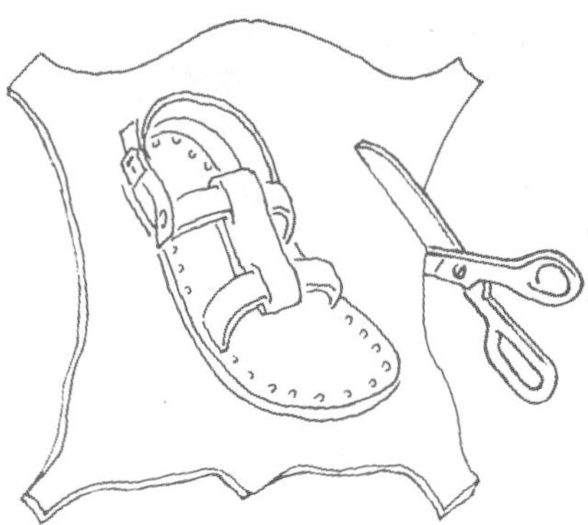

Most leatherwork can be completed with only four or five basic tools, some of which you probably already have around the house or workshop. Simple projects may only require a pair of scissors, razor cutter, or utility knife for cutting leather. But for others you'll probably need a hole punch, edge beveler, and perhaps a lacing needle and hammer. Many other leatherworking tools are available, but they're needed mainly to make your work easier, for special cutting jobs, or sewing leather.

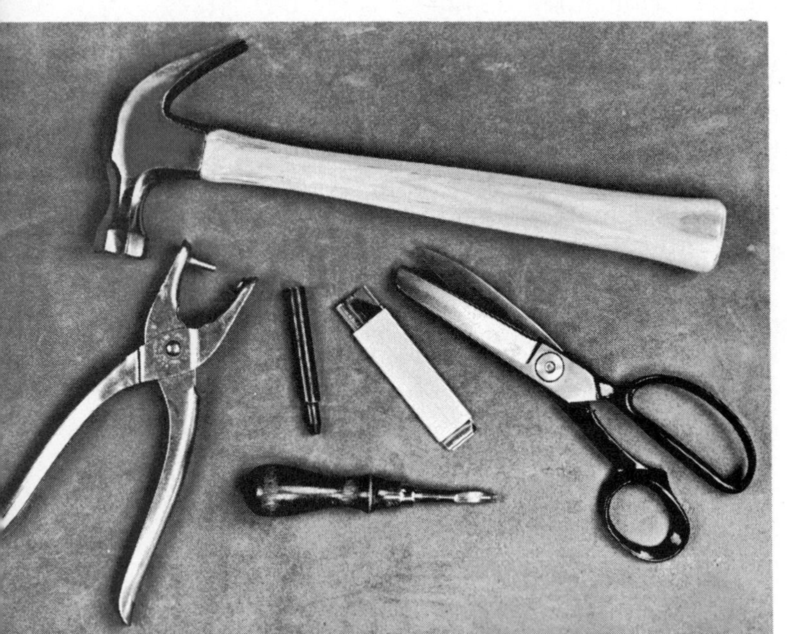

BASIC TOOLS (clockwise from top): hammer, leather shears, utility or razor knife, edge beveler, drive and spring punch.

A few common workshop tools are useful in leatherwork, mainly for measuring and marking: a steel straight edge or ruler for measuring and using as a guide for cutting with a knife; a T-square or 90° triangle for marking accurate square corners; an awl for scratching pattern outlines into leather and punching small sewing holes (page 16); and a flat metal pounding surface (a small anvil, a block of scrap iron, or even the side of a hammer will do) for setting rivets.

Before using any tool on an actual project, you should always give it a try on scrap leather to get a feel for how it works.

To avoid buying tools you don't need, look through pages 34-80 to find a project you'd like to make; in the instructions you'll find a list of the necessary tools.

Where can you buy tools for leatherworking? Leathercraft supply shops, hobby shops, and general craft supply stores usually carry them. So do leathercraft mail order houses (ask for catalogues at hobby and craft supply stores) and, occasionally, hardware stores.

FIVE BASIC TOOLS

Whether you're making a belt, a briefcase, or just a simple hair barrette, one or more of the following five basic tools is nearly always used: a pair of scissors, leather shears, or a utility knife (or razor cutter) to cut the leather with, an edge beveler, a hole punch, a hammer, and perhaps a lacing needle. You will be well prepared for most leatherwork if you start your tool collection with just a No. 5 round hole punch (page 13), a No. 3 edge beveler (page 15), and a utility or razor knife.

Something to Cut With

Unless you make a project from a kit that includes pre-cut pieces of leather, the most essential tool for all leather work is a pair of scissors, utility knife, razor cutter, or leather shears to cut the leather into shapes and sizes you want.

Household scissors. If strong and sharp, household or sewing scissors will cut through most thin leather (up to about 3 ounces). Trying to cut thicker leather with scissors, however, is difficult. The job is much easier with a utility or razor knife or leather shears.

Utility and razor knives. Inexpensive and good for almost all cutting jobs, a utility or razor knife will probably be your most frequently used tool. The simple razor blade type knife is especially handy. It carries a single-edge razor blade that retracts into the handle when you aren't using the knife. The blade is easily replaced when it becomes dull. (See page 21 for instructions on using knives.)

Leather shears. Designed for leather and other heavy materials, special leather shears are highly recommended by some craftsmen; others, however, still prefer to use a knife. Both knives and shears have advantages: the shears are best for cutting lightweight garment leather, while straight lines are most accurately cut with a knife and steel ruler. (See page 21.)

Hole and Slit Punches

Most projects require that some type of hole be punched in the leather for laces, rivets, grommets, eyelets, snaps, buckles, or sewing. Drive punches, spring punches, and thonging chisels are three tools designed for this purpose.

Drive punches. The least expensive type of punching tools are simply hollow metal tubes, sharpened at one end. To use one, hold the sharp end against the surface of the leather, then hit the other end with a hammer or mallet to drive the punch through. Always place a piece of soft material such as wood (with the end grain up), hard rubber, or a piece of thick linoleum beneath the leather where the tool will go through. Punching against any hard surface such as formica, metal, or concrete will immediately ruin the sharp end.

Round drive punches, used to punch holes for lacing, rivets, grommets, eyelets, and snaps, range in diameter from 1/16 on up to 1 inch and even larger. Sizes are indicated by numbers 0-15: the higher the number, the larger the diameter of the punch. A No. 5 (11/64 inch) punch is a good size for general work and will cut holes for large laces

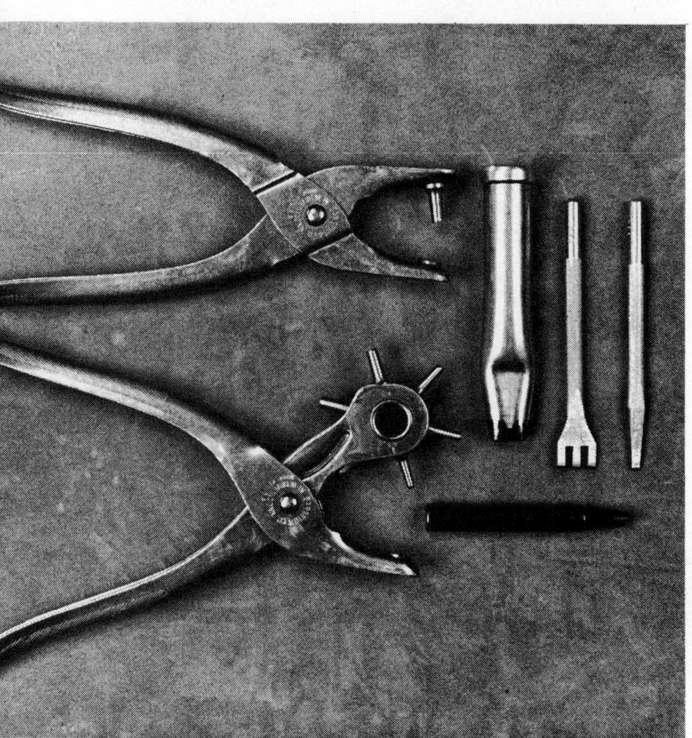

PUNCHING TOOLS (clockwise from bottom): rotary and spring punches, slot punch, thonging chisels, and drive punch.

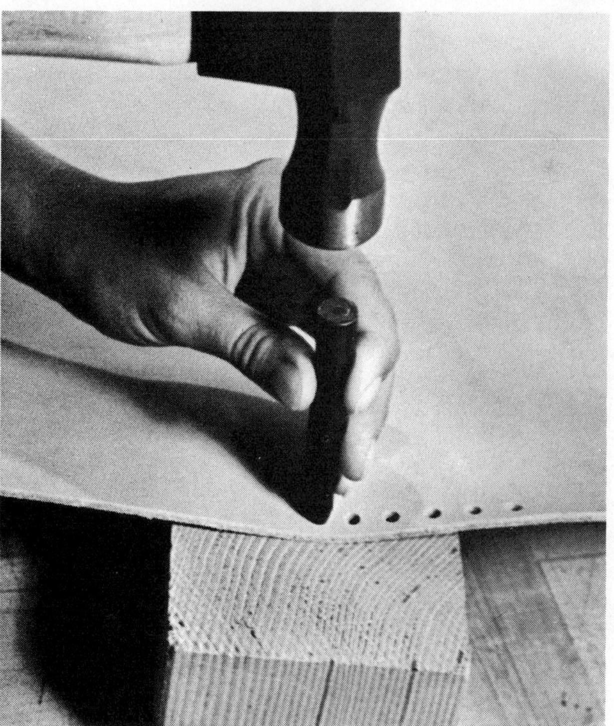

DRIVE PUNCHES are pounded through leather with a hammer, always against a soft surface such as wood.

SPRING PUNCHES have a punching tube attached to handles that are squeezed together to punch holes in leather.

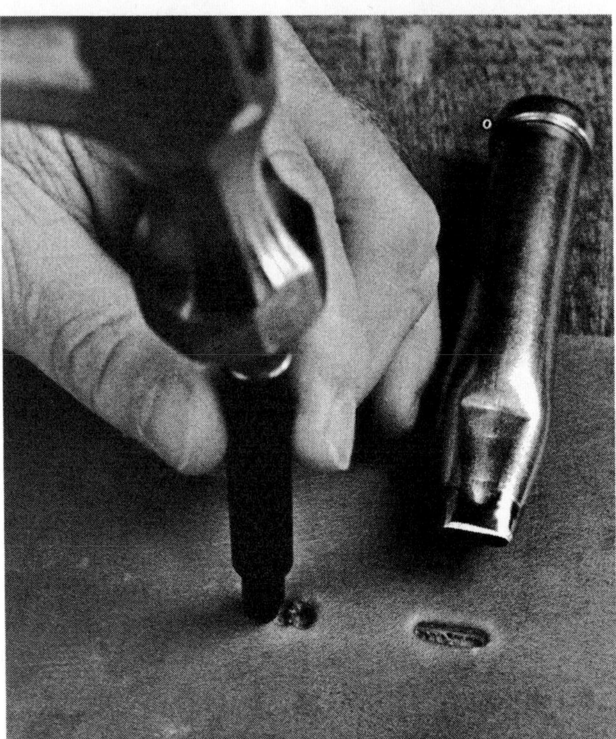

OBLONG HOLES can be made with a slot punch or by cutting a series of round holes with a drive punch.

and thongs, both large and small rivets, eyelets, and buckles—almost all the holes you will be making except those for thin laces which require either a No. 1 (3/32 inch diameter) punch or a thonging chisel (described below). An awl or a No. 0 punch makes holes for hand sewing.

Oblong holes can be cut in three ways: by punching a connected series of round holes, by punching two unconnected round holes and cutting out the middle with a knife, or by using an oval-shaped drive punch called a *slot* or *bag* punch. Slot punch sizes are ½, ⅝, ¾, and 1 inch long. Keep this point in mind when buying slot punches: a small punch can make larger holes if you cut two overlapping holes, but a large tool can't be used to make smaller holes.

Spring punches. Somewhat more convenient than drive punches, spring punches are plier-like tools with a punching tube and soft metal anvil attached to the head. All you do is place the leather between the punching tube and small metal anvil which is beneath it and squeeze the handles together. One drawback of spring punches, however, is that you can't use them to make holes more than a few inches away from the edge of the leather because the handles get in the way. To make holes in the middle of a piece of leather, you'll need a drive punch.

Round punching tubes for spring punches are available from Nos. 0-7 (1/16-13/64 inch diameters) and can be removed from the handles with a wrench so that the same spring punch can be used to cut different-sized holes. Some tool companies also make thonging chisel attachments and eyelet setters (page 28) for spring punches. Cutting different sizes and kinds of holes with the same tool, however, damages the soft metal anvil, which then must either be filed flat again or replaced with a new one.

To help save both the punching tube and the anvil, place a piece of scrap leather between the anvil and leather you are punching through.

Rotary spring punches. Rather than just a single punching tube, rotary spring punches have a number of different-sized tubes attached to a head that is turned when you want to punch holes of different sizes. Although the rotary punch seems to be an especially convenient tool, the spring and ratchet mechanism that fixes the tubes in punching position tends to wear out quickly in all but expensive models, causing uneven holes.

Thonging chisels. Slits in leather for lacing with flat calf lace (page 22) can be punched with a thonging chisel. A small round hole punch (No. 0 or 1) also will work for these laces, but slits keep them flat and right side up.

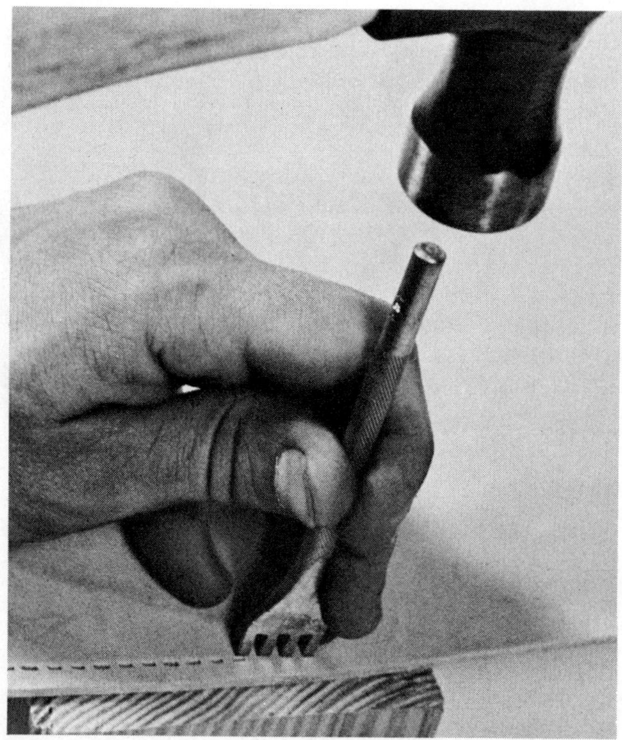

MULTIPLE-PRONGED thonging chisel is used to cut a long series of slits along edges of leather for flat laces.

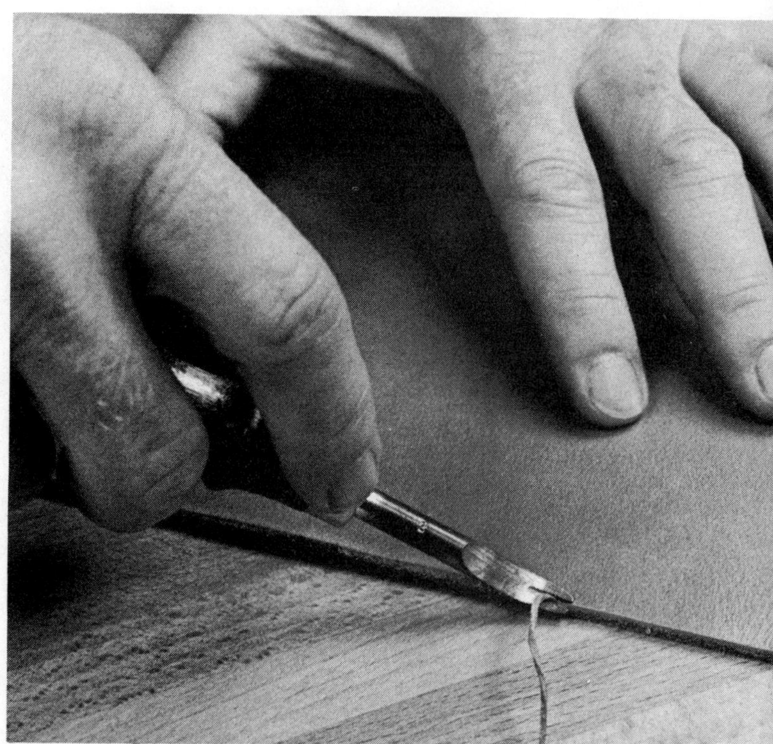

EDGE BEVELER cuts off a thin strip from square-sided edges of thick leather, leaving them smoothly rounded.

Multiple-pronged thonging chisels help in cutting a long series of slits. But to go around corners or cut odd numbers of slits, a single-prong chisel is needed. Since slits cut with a thonging chisel usually run parallel to the edge of the leather, thonging chisels can only be used to make slits for lacing stitches that go over the edges, not those that run parallel to the edges.

Pound a thonging chisel through the leather with a hammer or mallet, always against a soft-surface base (end grain wood is best), just as you would a drive punch. When making a series of slits with a multiple-pronged thonging chisel, assure equal spacing by putting the end prong into the last slit of the set just completed.

Prongs come in two widths, so be sure to get a thonging chisel with prongs that match the size of the lace you are using, usually either 3/32 or ⅛ inch wide.

Edge Beveler

An edge beveler cuts off a thin strip of leather along edges, making them smoothly rounded. Although beveling isn't essential, it gives otherwise square-sided edges an attractive tapered finish and helps prevent them from fraying and curling with wear. Both sides of edges are usually beveled, but sides visible or exposed to wear are the most important to bevel. Edges of thin or sueded leather are not usually beveled.

To bevel an edge, lay the leather flat on a steady surface with the side to be beveled facing up. Place the V-shaped notch in the tip of the beveler against the edge and, keeping the handle at a 45° angle, push forward to cut off a thin sliver of leather. Try not to tilt the beveler too much to one side; this may cause an uneven cut or gouge the surface of the leather. Don't worry when using an edge beveler, you can't easily hurt yourself on the blade nor cut off too much leather. Just be sure to keep your fingers away from the edge of the leather you are working on.

A steady, continuous cutting action is best, but if the leather starts bunching up in front of the blade, stop and move the tool back an inch or so before continuing. If the leather bunches up frequently or if the beveler cuts only with difficulty, you'll know that it is probably dull. Sharpen bevelers as described on page 19.

Bevelers come in sizes 1-5, indicating the width of the V in the tip of the blade. The larger the V is, the more leather the tool cuts off. Use low-numbered bevelers for thin leather; bevelers with high numbers for thick leather. For general, all-around work, select a No. 2 or 3 beveler.

Hammer

A hammer or mallet is necessary for pounding drive punches, thonging chisels, and stamping dies (page 32), for setting rivets and for flattening seams that have been sewn, laced, or glued. Any ordinary workshop hammer will do, though a rawhide or hickory mallet, available in a variety of sizes and weights, won't wear the ends of tools as much as a steel hammer will.

Lacing Needle

Although you can lace projects without a lacing needle, using one makes the job much easier by giving the lace a rigid end that can be forced through lacing holes and used to line up uneven holes.

Two types of lacing needles are available. One is hollow, and threaded on the inside at one end so that the lace can be screwed part way into it. The needle's point is blunt to prevent snagging as it is pushed through lacing holes. If you have difficulty fitting the lace into the needle cut the end to a tapering point then burn it with a match until it hardens.

The other lacing needle is split into two barbed prongs at one end. The end of the lace is placed between the prongs, which are squeezed together, forcing the barbs into the lace.

SEWING TOOLS

Leather can be sewn by hand or on a sewing machine. For hand-sewing leather, you'll need several tools, the most important of which are needles and thread. All hand and machine sewing instructions are described on pages 24-26.

Needles and Thread

Thin leather, up to about 3 or 4 ounces or so, can be hand sewn with a sharp *glover's needle,* which has a three-sided point to prevent binding as it pierces through the leather. Because thicker kinds of leather are more difficult to pierce with a needle, holes for the stitches are made first with an awl or No. 0 round hole punch, and the thread is pulled through them with a blunt *harness needle.*

Cotton-wrapped polyester thread is recommended for sewing garment and other lightweight

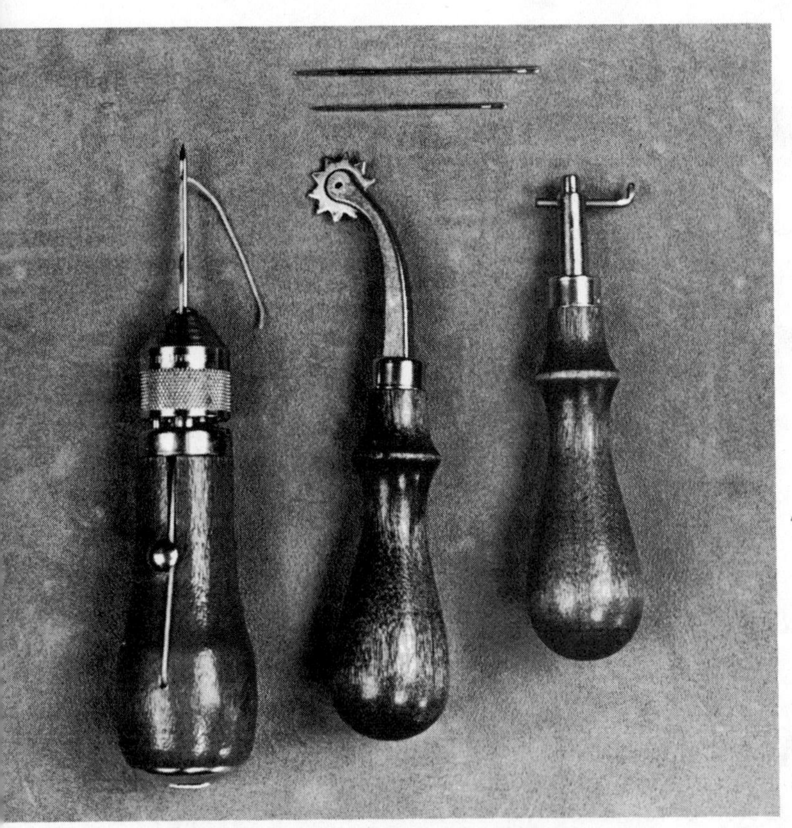

SEWING TOOLS: include harness and glover's needles (top), stitching awl (left), stitch marker, and groover (right).

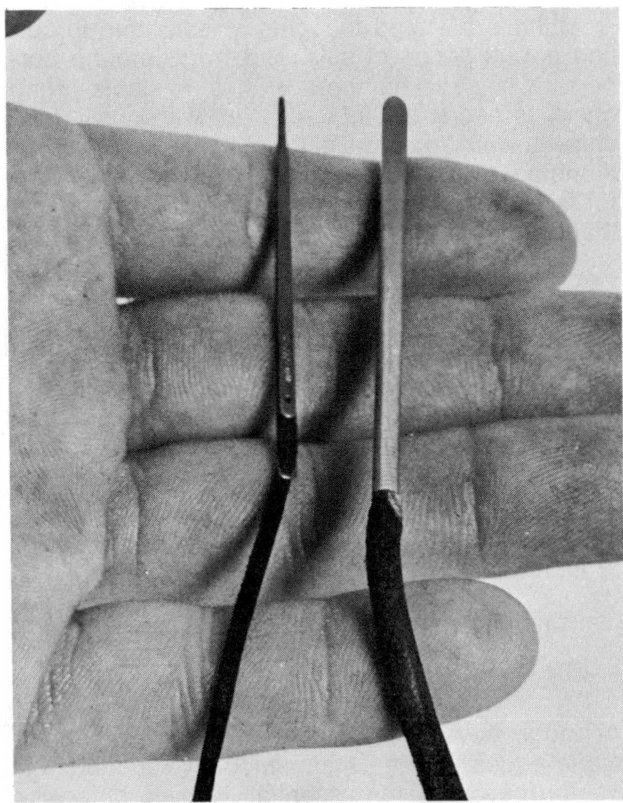

FOR EASY LACING use a pronged lacing needle with calf lace (left) and a round needle with thongs (right).

leather. Three- or five-cord waxed nylon thread is strong enough to hold heavier leather.

If you plan to do much hand sewing or sew long seams, an *automatic stitching awl* or *hand stitcher* will be very helpful. The automatic stitcher produces a strong locking stitch; the wooden handle and heavy duty needle make piercing through thick leather easy.

Stitch Marker

The stitch marker makes it easier to space hand-sewn stitches (and sandal sole tacks) correctly. As you push the tool along the surface of the leather, the small star or spur-shaped wheel makes 5, 6, or 7 (depending on the tool) equally spaced indentations per inch. If you lift the stitch marker up off the leather in the middle of a seam, be sure to replace it so that one of the points of the wheel is in a previous indentation. Stitch markers will not work on soft, sueded leather.

Stitching Groover

To make your stitches lie flush with the surface of thick leather rather than rest on top of it, you can cut a shallow groove in the leather along the stitching line. The stitching groover is designed for this purpose. To use it, first adjust the cutting tube so that its end is the same distance from the shaft of the tool as you want the stitch line to be from the edge of the leather. (A small screw in the tip of the tool's shaft holds the tube in place.) Next, place the end of the stitch groover against the edge of the leather and, with the cutting tube pressed into the surface, pull it towards you.

SPECIAL CUTTING TOOLS

The razor knife, scissors, and leather shears described on page 13 are suitable for most of the cutting you'll have to do. But for more specialized leatherwork, several other cutting tools are helpful: the skiving knife, draw gauge, and V-gouge.

Skiving Knife

Edges of thick leather that must be folded under or joined without creating a bulky seam can be trimmed to a more workable thickness with a skiving knife.

COUNTERSINK STITCHES in thick leather by cutting a groove along stitch lines with a stitching groover.

INDENTATIONS in leather left by a stitch marker make it easy to evenly space sewn stitches, sandal sole tacks.

Two kinds of skiving knives are available. One is basically just a sharp knife. To use it, place the leather flat on a steady surface and pare away the surface. The angle of the blade to the surface of the leather determines how much leather is sliced off: the wider the angle, the deeper the knife will cut.

The other kind of skiving knife, called a safety beveler, has a razor blade in a curved holder that prevents it from cutting too deeply. The knife works just like a vegetable peeler.

Whichever type of skiving knife you use, slice off only a thin layer of leather at a time to avoid cutting the piece too thin. (As in the case of haircuts, it's easier to take off more later than to replace what's already been cut.) Skive the backside (flesh side) of the leather, rather than the front surface (grain side). That way, if you make a mistake, the visible side of the leather will still be presentable.

The skiving knife can also be used to shave off a thin layer from the grain side of leather when another piece is to be glued to it. The coarser surface that results holds the glue better than a smooth one.

Draw Gauge

Straps and "belt blanks" (strips of leather used to make belts) can be cut from a large piece of leather with a razor cutter and straight edge (page 21), or a draw gauge. Several kinds of draw gauges are available. The best is one which has two bars that adjust to the thickness of the leather and support it both on top and bottom while you use the tool. The blade is held in between these bars. Other kinds of draw gauges have only one bar that holds the blade and leaves it dangerously exposed. Extreme caution is needed while using the tool or else the leather will buckle or the blade dive into the leather and produce an uneven cut.

To use a draw gauge, first set the distance between the blade and the side of the handle (which acts as a guide) to the width you want the strap to be. Then, starting at one end of the piece of leather, place the handle firmly against the edge of the leather, and pull the tool towards you. Remember: the draw gauge will make a straight cut only if the edge of leather that the guide follows is straight to begin with.

V-Gouges

When thick, stiff leather must be folded, a V-gouge is used to make a narrow V-shaped cut along the fold line. Several types of V-gouges are available: some operate like a woodworking plane and have a

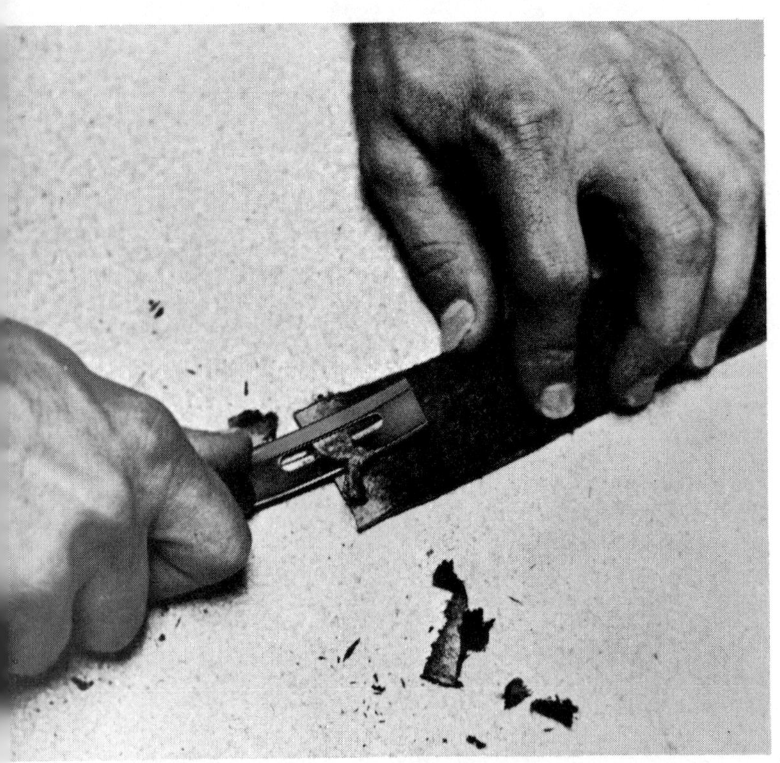

THICK LEATHER can be thinned down with skiving knife that pares the surface like a vegetable peeler.

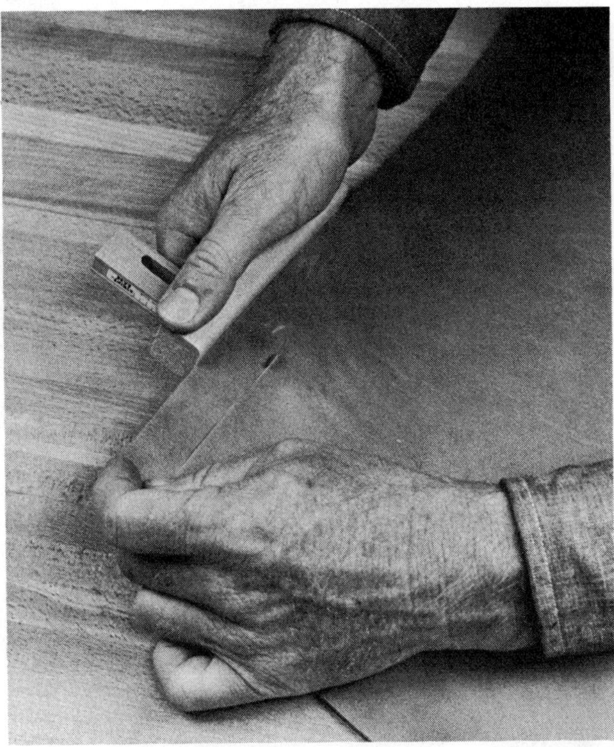

STRAPS AND BELTS can be cut with a draw gauge, but use care with models having an exposed blade as this one does.

fully adjustable blade; others work like a chisel and must be controlled by hand.

TOOL CARE

When tools are treated reasonably well and not used on materials or for jobs they aren't intended for, sharpening is the only necessary care.

Scissors can be sharpened on a home knife-sharpener, grinder, or whet stone. But special leather shears with a serrated lower blade should be sharpened by a professional.

If bevelers and hole punches aren't too dull, they can be sharpened with fine grit (No. 600) emery paper. To sharpen an edge beveler, fold the paper and draw the tip of the tool back and forth over the crease. For the inside of a hole punch, roll the emery paper into a cylinder or around a pencil and push it in and out of the punch. The outside of the punch can be sharpened on a grinder or whet stone or with a file.

Chips and nicks in the cutting edge of a tool will have to be filed or ground out on a grinding wheel before you give the edge a final sharpening.

Light rust on the surface of metal tools can usually be removed by sanding lightly with fine grit emery paper.

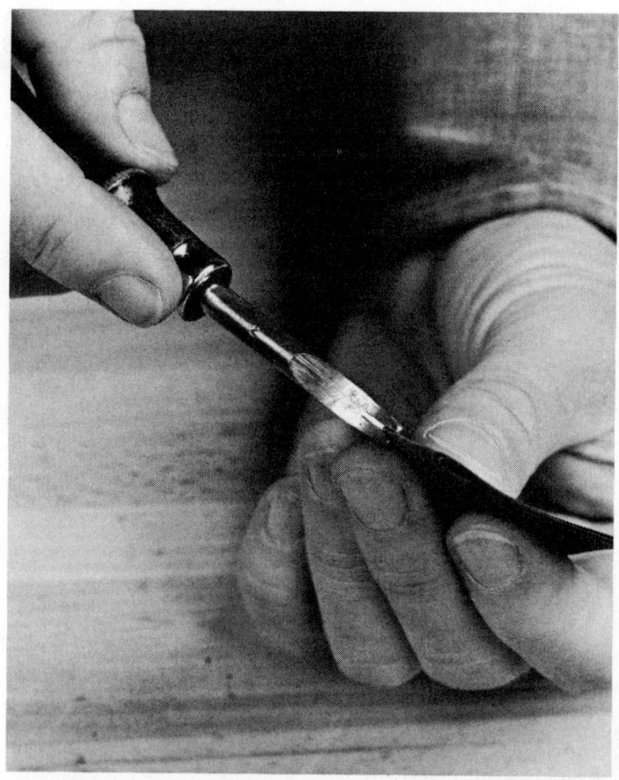

SHARPEN an edge beveler by drawing the V in the tip of the tool across a folded piece of emery paper.

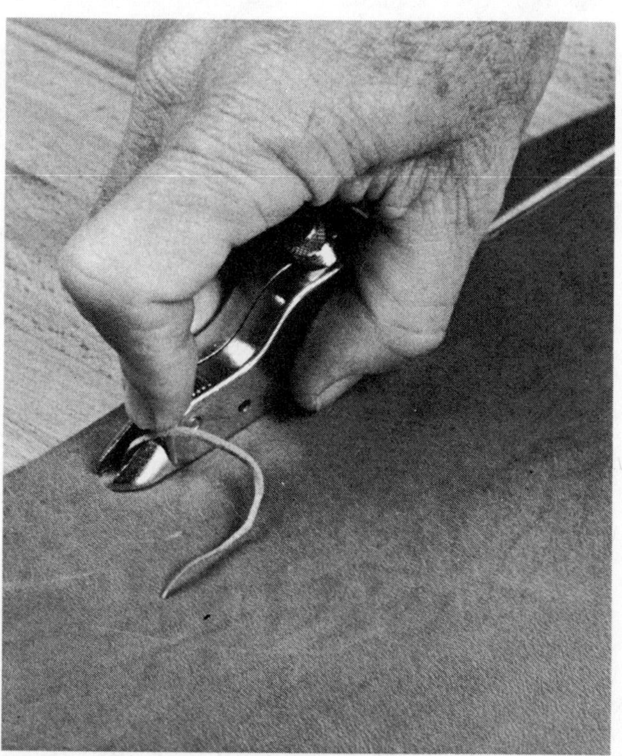

BLADE in the tip of this wood-plane type V-gouge cuts a V in thick leather, allowing it to be folded easily.

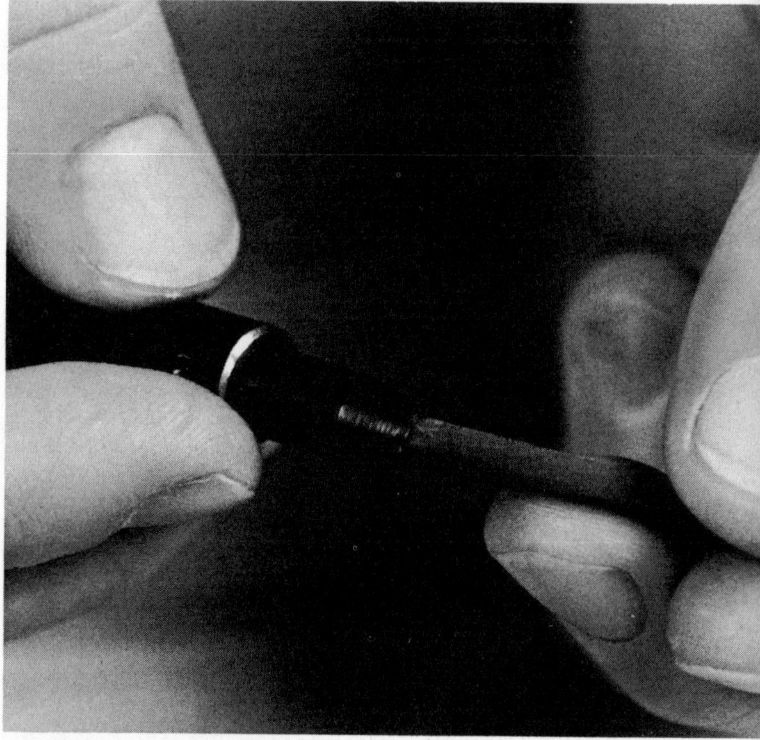

DRIVE PUNCHES are sharpened with fine-grit emery paper. To treat inside edge, roll the paper into a tube.

LEATHERCRAFT TECHNIQUES

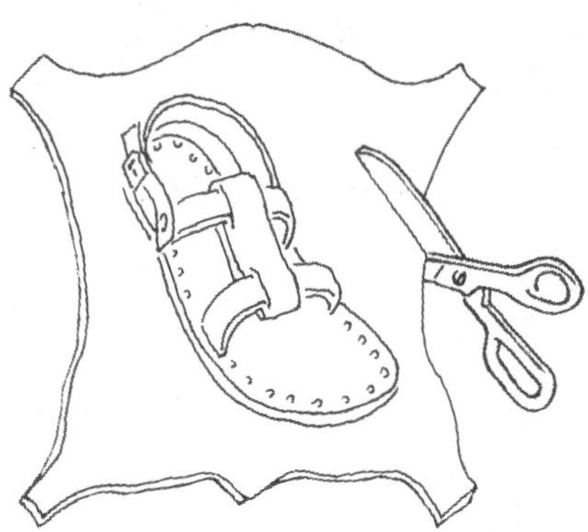

The techniques used in leatherworking are not difficult. You can begin to make useful things—even a handbag, briefcase, or pair of sandals—without previous experience.

Cutting leather and joining pieces together are the steps you'll repeat most often and can be picked up as you are making things. Other techniques, such as dyeing leather and decorating, take trial-and error practice. After some experimenting on scrap, however, you'll be ready to tackle a project. Of course, your work will improve with experience, but the primary ingredients of success are patience and care.

PATTERNS AND CUTTING

After deciding what to make, the first step is to cut leather into the right shapes and sizes. Some projects, such as watchbands and belts, are simple enough that measurements for the different parts can be transferred directly onto the leather and then cut out. Others are trickier however, especially if two or more curved pieces of leather are involved. In these cases you normally need to prepare and follow a pattern, to avoid expensive cutting errors.

Patterns

Descriptions of most of the projects on pages 34-80 include instructions for making the necessary pattern.

Patterns for garments are available in fabric stores and fashion magazines. Those designed for heavy fabrics can most easily be adapted to leather. Simple patterns without pleats, gathers, or folds are best.

If you have an idea for a project not included in this book and need to make a pattern for it, first draw a rough sketch of the article and determine how many separate pieces of leather are needed, their sizes and shapes, and the way they'll be held together. (See pages 21-28 for methods of joining leather.) Keeping seams, rivets, lacing, and any other fittings in mind, draw a full-sized outline of each part on heavy paper or pattern paper, then cut them out.

To make sure the parts fit properly and the completed project will look the way you've planned, assemble the paper pattern with staples, masking tape, or paper clips. (Be sure to allow for seams and any other fittings that will be added on the actual project.) Adjustments and alterations, if any, should be made in the pattern before you transfer measurements onto the leather.

When the appearance of the paper model satisfies you, take it apart, being careful not to tear any of the pieces. Lay the pattern pieces out flat on the leather, and tape them down with masking tape. (Never use pins to hold a pattern to leather because they will leave noticeable holes in the leather.)

When positioning the pattern on leather, try to place the pieces so as to avoid any scars, scratches, and holes in the skin unless they will enhance the project.

Trace around each part of the pattern with a soft-lead pencil or tailor's chalk. If you don't bear down too hard on the leather while tracing, pencil mistakes can be erased; chalk just rubs off. Tracing is easiest if you glue the pattern to stiff cardboard and then cut it out again. After drawing completely

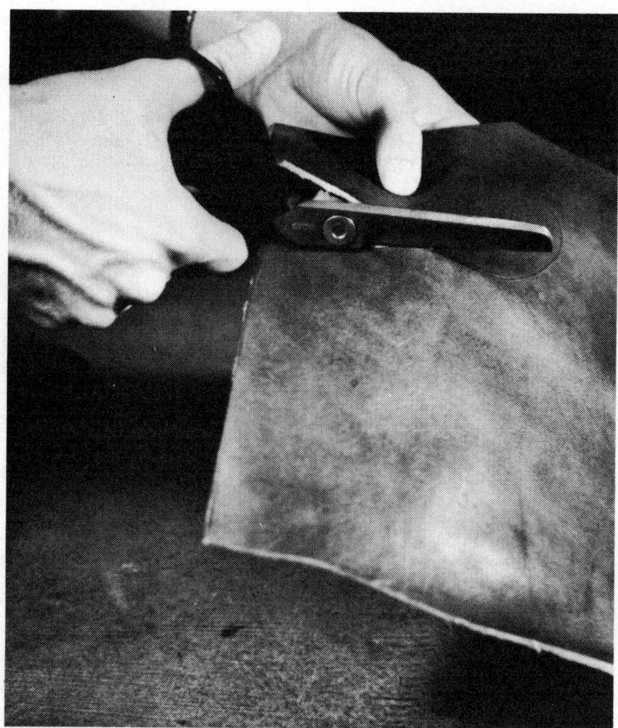

HEAVY-DUTY leather shears work like scissors and easily cut almost any kind or thickness of leather.

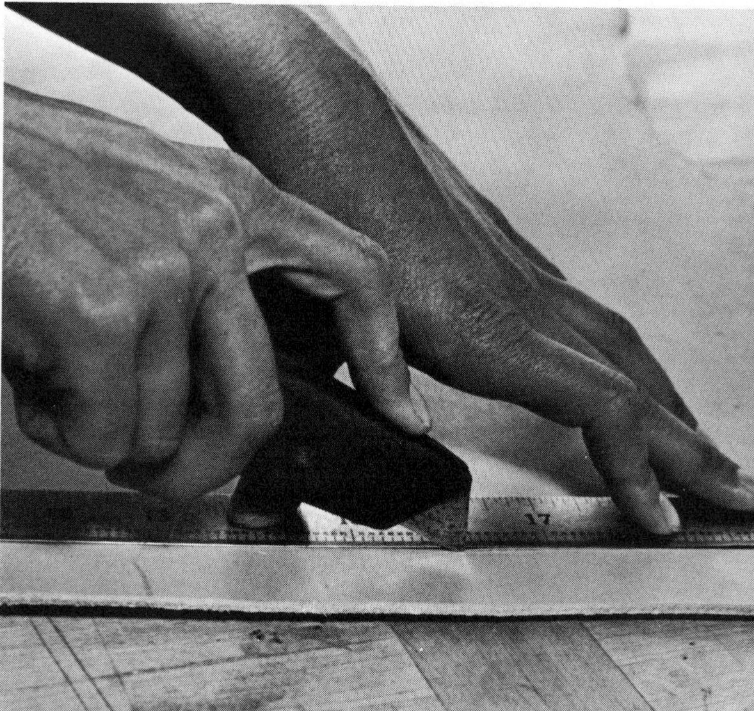

RAZOR OR UTILITY KNIFE cuts most leathers. Use a steel ruler to guide blade when cutting straight lines.

around each part, remove the pattern and you'll be ready to cut the leather.

Cutting Leather

Cut leather with scissors, leather shears, or a razor or utility knife (pages 12 and 13). If you use scissors or shears, cut around the outline of each part as you would any other fabric, supporting the leather with one hand and cutting with the other.

To cut leather with a razor-type knife, first lay the leather out flat on a table top or other steady surface. Press the point of the blade into the surface of the leather and pull the knife along the outline of the shape you want. A piece of linoleum or pressed fiberboard makes a good cutting surface. Never cut against hard surfaces such as formica or metal since this will damage the blade.

Straight lines are most accurately cut if you use a steel ruler or straight edge as a guide for the knife blade as shown in the photograph. When cutting round or curved shapes with a knife, turn the leather as necessary so that your hand always moves in a comfortable direction.

Never force the knife to slice all the way through hard, thick leather on the first try. Instead, cut only part way through at first, repeating the cut as many times as necessary to finish. (Remember: knives are sharp; the more pressure applied when cutting, the less control you have over the blade and the easier it is to make mistakes or hurt yourself.)

PUTTING IT TOGETHER

The final appearance of any project depends just as much on how it is fastened together as on the kind of leather and the shapes of the different pieces. Choosing an appropriate means of fastening is therefore one of your primary concerns. Riveting, lacing, sewing, and gluing are the most common methods, each creating a different effect. You may also have use for findings and fastenings such as snaps, harness buttons, grommets, and eyelets on projects like purses which are opened and closed frequently.

Riveting

Though associated more with steel and heavy machinery than with leather, riveting is one of the easiest and strongest ways of holding pieces of leather together. Rivets are most effective for securing narrow pieces, such as straps, or for giving extra strength to ends of seams that have been sewn or laced. Since rivets give projects a sturdy appearance, they are a natural for casual sorts of projects

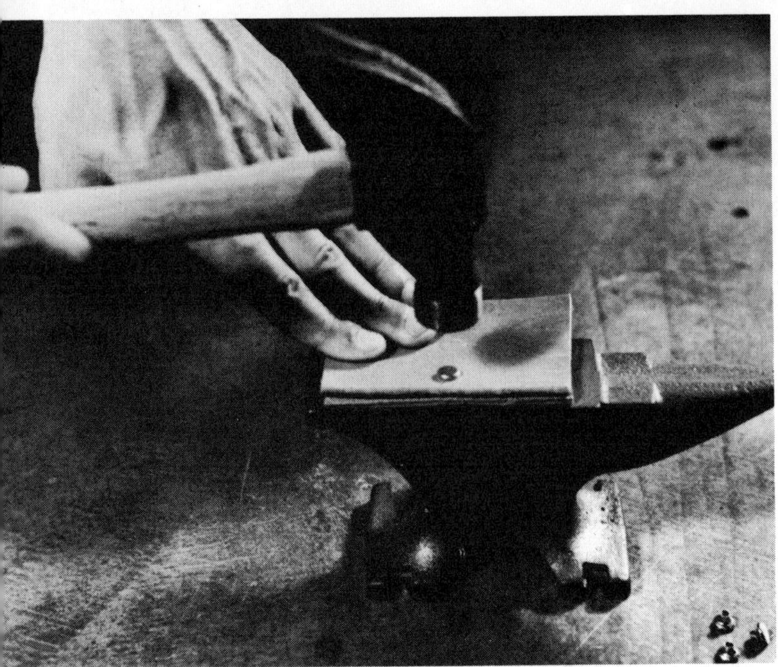

SET RIVETS by pounding the cap flat over the stem, against a hard, flat surface such as a small anvil.

and thick leather. Two or more rivets frequently are arranged in a project to create a decorative pattern or design.

Rivets are available in several sizes. Two-part rivets—consisting of a stem and a cap—are the strongest kind. When properly set, they'll hold until the leather wears out. Rivets with either a 1/4- or 5/8-inch diameter are most frequently used.

To set a rivet, first punch a hole in both pieces of leather at the point where you want the rivet to go. Then insert the stem part through both holes from the underside of the leather and place the cap over it.

With the stem side against a hard flat surface, such as a piece of steel or iron (the side of a hammer head will do—but never brick, concrete, or formica), hit the cap hard with a hammer to smash it flat. This causes the stem to mushroom up into the hollow part of the cap; at the same time, the cap is flattened, locking the two parts together. You may have to hit the rivet two or three times to assure that it is well set. Don't be afraid of striking the cap fairly hard—a dented or broken rivet can be replaced, but one that isn't well set might pull apart at any time.

For the rivet to look its best, try not to dent the cap: hit it squarely and flatly with the center of the hammer head. A rivet setter may be helpful. One end of the setter is concave, fitting over the rounded cap of the rivet. When the other end is hit with a hammer, the cap is forced down over the stem but not completely flattened.

Dented rivets can be removed by driving a nail or nail setter through the cap. This splits the stem so that it can be pulled free of the cap.

Before trying to rivet your project, practice setting a few rivets on scrap leather.

Lacing

Lacing involves threading long narrow strips of leather through holes or slits in the leather and is the easiest way to hold edges of two or more pieces of leather together in a long seam. Lacing gives projects a sturdy, hand-crafted appearance.

Lacing and lacing tools. To lace a project, you'll need a hole punch or thonging chisel to make the lacing holes, a lacing needle, and, of course, the laces. Hole punching tools and lacing needles are described on pages 13-16; which of them you'll use depends upon the kind of lace you decide on. Although many different kinds of laces are available, thongs and calf lace are by far the greatest favorites and are standard items in leather shops and craft stores. An alternative to buying pre-cut lace (sold by the yard) is to cut your own lace. To do this just cut a piece of the leather you want to use into a circle, then with a knife or leather shears begin cutting a strip the width you want the lace to be. Continue cutting all the way around the circle in a spiral.

- *Leather thongs,* made out of cowhide, are squarish, from 5/32 to 3/16 inch wide, and are usually used to lace projects made out of thick leather (5 ounces and over). Thongs come in a variety of colors and neutral yellow or tan that can be dyed to match the rest of your project. Cut lacing holes for thongs with a No. 5 round hole punch (see page 13). A round hollow lacing needle is usually used with thongs.
- *Calf lace* is flattish—the outer side slightly rounded with a smooth, shiny finish. Calf laces are best for thin leather (under 4 ounces), small projects, and when flat and non-bulky seams are required. The most popular sizes, 3/32 and 1/8 inch wide, are available in colors as well as in neutral tan. Thread calf lace through slits made with a thonging chisel or small holes cut with a No. 0 or 1 round hole punch. (Slits can only be used if the lacing stitch goes over the edge of the leather.)

Lacing stitches. All of the lacing stitches described below require holes or slits (depending on the kind of lace and stitch) for the laces to be threaded through: one hole in both pieces of leather for every stitch you want to make. Lacing holes for any stitch (whip stitch, cordovan stitch) that goes over the edges of the leather or is perpendicular to it can be made with either the hole punch or thonging chisel. Stitches that run parallel to the edge but do not go over it must be made through holes cut with a round hole punch, since the thonging chisel only cuts slits running parallel to the edge.

The amount of space between the holes and their distance from the edge of the leather depends on how you want the lacing to look. Spacing should, however, be consistent so that the holes coincide when the pieces of leather are placed together. When deciding on spacing, consider the size of the lace and type of stitches you're going to use. Laced seams will be less bulky if lightly hammered flat after completion.

• *Single running stitches* are made by simply drawing the lace through each successive pair of holes, pulling it tight as you go. Before starting, tie a knot in the end of the lace to keep it from going all the way through the first holes. A knot in the other end after you've finished will prevent the lace from coming undone. This stitch requires a length of lace that is about 1½ times longer than the seam.

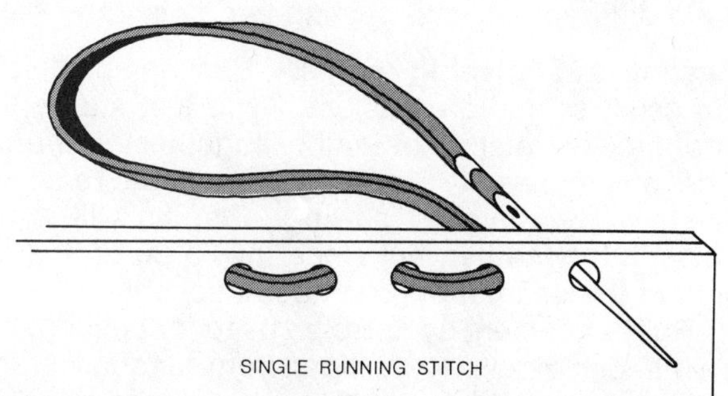

SINGLE RUNNING STITCHES are made by pulling the lace through each successive hole in the leather.

If you want the knots to end up on the same side of the seam, cut an even number of lacing holes. The purse on pages 48 and 49 was laced with the single running stitch.

• *Double running stitches* are made in exactly the same way as the single running stitch except that after going through the last set of holes, you continue lacing back around in the opposite direction, going through each pair of holes a second time. When you reach the holes you started with, tie the ends of the lace together. About twice as much lace is needed as for the single running stitch.

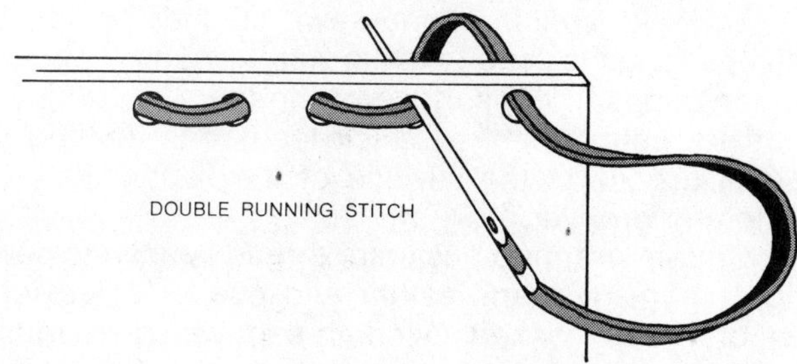

DOUBLE RUNNING STITCHES are the single version, continued in the opposite direction after completing the last hole.

• *Whip stitches* are made by passing the end of the lace through the first set of holes, over the edge of the seam, and then through the second pair of holes. Continue lacing in this "through, over, and through" fashion to the end of the seam. A length of lace that is three times the distance to be laced will be needed.

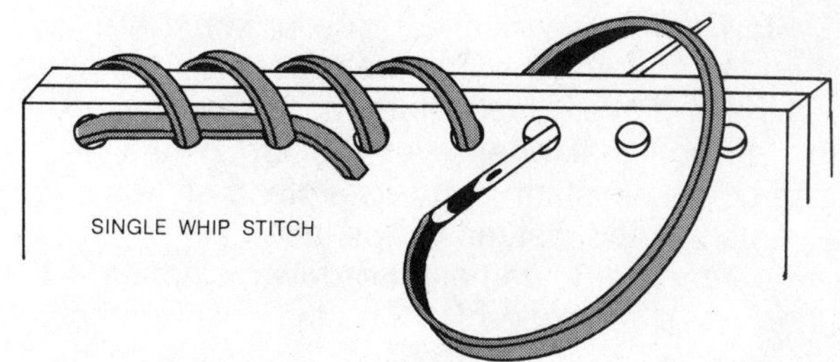

TO MAKE WHIP stitches, put the lace end through the first hole, over the edge, and through the next hole.

• *Double whip stitches* involve the same "over and through" stitches of the single whip stitch, except instead of going directly from one hole to the next, you lace through each hole twice. You'll need twice as much lace for this stitch as you would for the single running stitch.

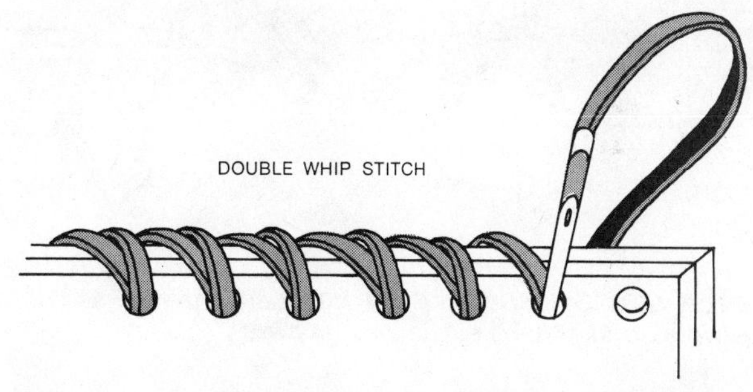

DOUBLE WHIP STITCHES are the same as the single version, except that you go through each hole twice.

Whip stitches can be kept from coming undone in several ways. Tying knots in the ends of the lace is the easiest. Another method is to pull the lace all the way through the first holes until only a short length of the end remains on one side. Bend this end against the leather in the direction you are lacing and make the second and third stitches over it. Finish the seam by pulling the end of the lace back under the last several stitches.

A third method of beginning and finishing whip stitches is to pull the lace through the first and last holes twice, then cut the ends off close.

When whip stitching completely around a project, join the ends in the following manner: when you reach the last 2 or 3 holes, bend the starting end of the lace against the unlaced section, then continue lacing over it with the other end. After going through the starting set of holes a second time, pull the end of the lace under the first 2 or 3 stitches and cut it off.

• *Single cordovan, or button hole stitches* cover the edges of the leather with a decorative pattern of the lace. (An example is seen in the billfold on page 47.)

Start cordovan stitches as you would the whip stitch. After going through the second pair of holes, pull the end over, back under, and through the section of lace that goes over the top of the seam. (The cordovan stitch requires a piece of lace about seven times the distance to be laced.)

You can begin and end cordovan stitches in the same ways described for the single whip stitch. If the beginning and end of the lacing are to meet, join the ends by pulling out the first stitch that was made. Then, after lacing through the last set of holes, take the end of the lace through the loop created by pulling out the first stitch. Now thread the end through the last set of holes a second time.

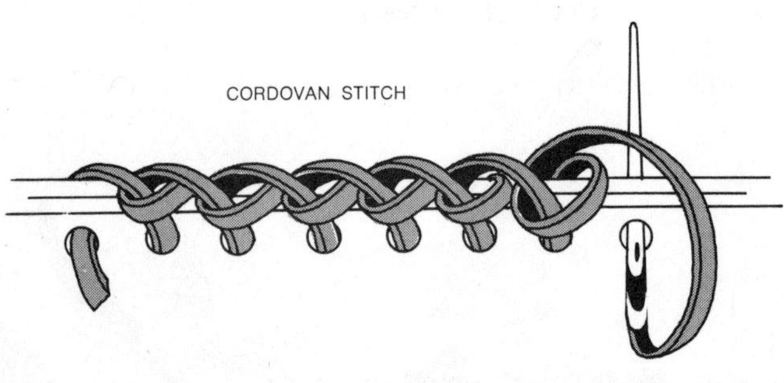

AFTER GOING UNDER the last stitch, pull the lace tight and continue through the next hole in leather.

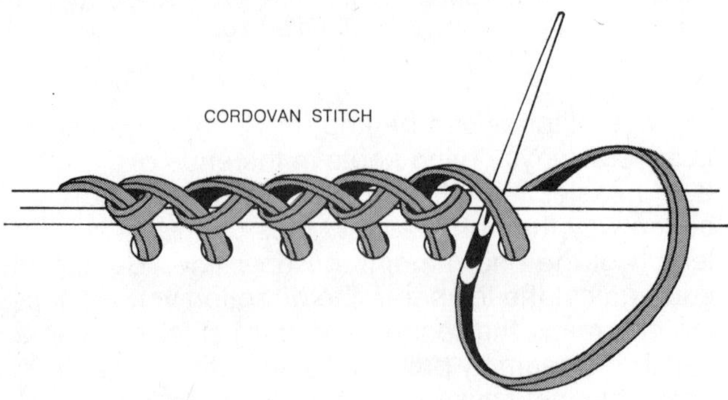

CORDOVAN STITCHES are like whip stitches except that the lace end is pulled under each previous stitch.

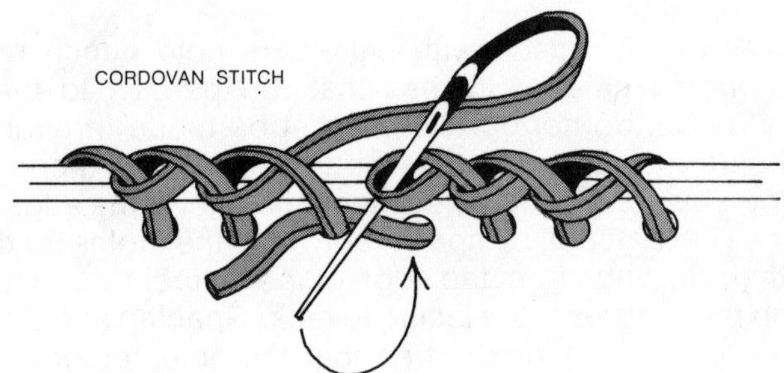

JOIN ENDS of cordovan stitch by pulling out the first stitch and passing lace end through newly created loop.

SEWING LEATHER

Since laces are rather thick and rivets are metallic, both become a very noticeable part of any project. Sewing, like lacing and riveting, is another way of holding projects together, but since thread is thin and non-bulky, sewing produces a much smoother, finer seam.

Leather is sewn either by hand or on a sewing machine, in the same way as any other fabric. The main difference lies in basting and finishing.

Basting and finishing seams. Basting and finishing sewn seams are easiest if you just staple the edges of the pieces of leather together on the inside of the seam. Staples can just be removed when you've finished sewing. Staples will make holes in the leather, but since they'll be on the inside of the seam they won't be noticeable.

Rubber cement can also be used for basting, but it is almost impossible to clean from sueded leather.

Completed seams can either be left the way they are or you can fold the seam allowance over and sew it down to create a flat-felled seam.

Hand sewing. There are several ways of hand sewing leather; tools and equipment are described on pages 16 and 17.

If the leather is thin or soft enough to pierce easily, a sharp glover's needle can be used. Otherwise, punch small holes with an awl or No. 0 round hole punch where the stitches are to be made, and pull the thread through them with a blunt harness needle. A third way of hand sewing is with an automatic stitching awl.

To make spacing hand-sewn stitches easier, a stitch marker is used to make small, equally spaced indentations in the surface of the leather. Stitches can be countersunk in thick leather by cutting a small groove in the surface of the leather with a stitching groover.

Cotton-wrapped polyester thread is used to sew lightweight garment leather and suedes. Heavier, 3- or 5-cord waxed nylon thread will hold thick leather.

Stitches used for hand sewing leather are the same for both the glover's needle and harness needle; follow the special instructions for using the stitching awl.

• *Running stitches* and *whip stitches* for sewing are made as described for lacing on pages 23 and 24. A stronger seam with both stitches is created by doubling back and sewing a second time as described for the double running and double whip stitches.

• *Back stitches* are similar to running stitches, except that instead of sewing each stitch directly in front of the previous one, you drop back to the last hole and go through it a second time before sewing forward again.

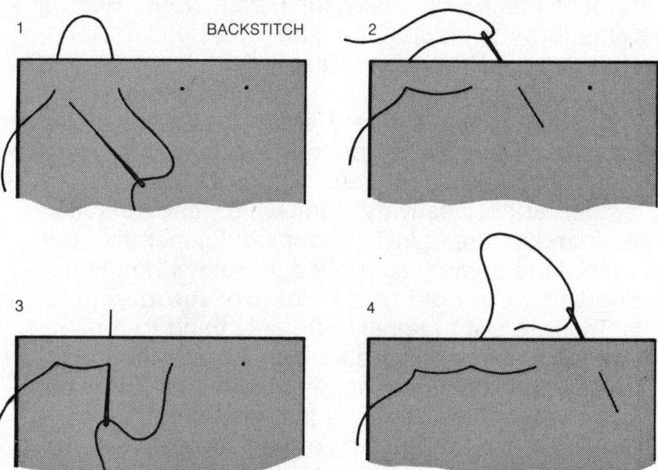

START BACKSTITCHES like running stitches but drop back to previous stitch before continuing foreward.

• *The automatic stitching awl* is extremely helpful for hand-sewing long seams. It makes a strong locked stitch similar to a sewing machine and carries a spool of thread in the handle which feeds out as you sew.

To operate an automatic stitcher, first put the end of the thread through the eye in the point of the needle; then pierce the leather and pull the thread all the way through to the other side. This end acts as bobbin thread for the stitches and should be about twice as long as the distance to be sewn.

Push the needle through the leather where the next stitch is to be made, drawing it halfway out again to create a loop in the thread along the needle. Pass the end of the bobbin thread through this loop and withdraw the needle from the leather completely. Both ends of the thread are then pulled equally tight so that the loop between the bobbin thread and needle thread lies *between* the pieces of leather, not flat along the surface.

Sewing with a machine. Lightweight leather and suedes (1½-3 ounces) can be sewn on most home sewing machines. A medium-sized needle (size 16-

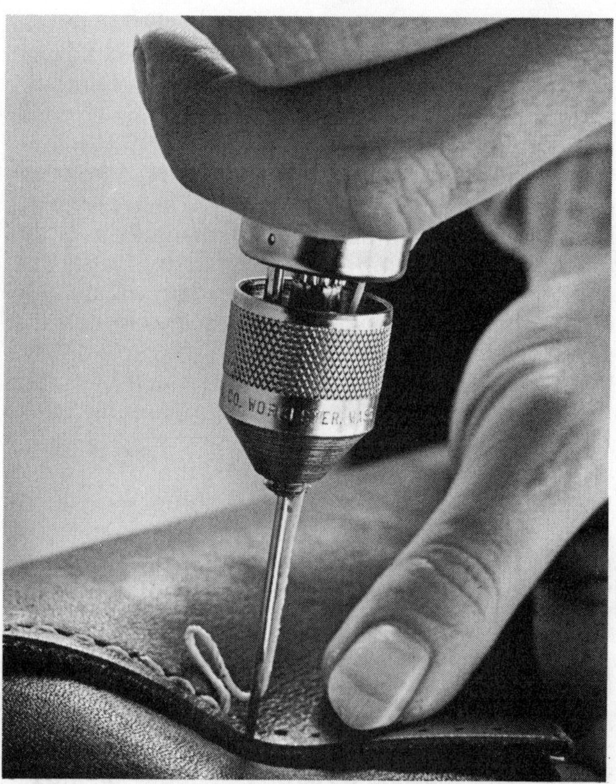

TO WORK a stitching awl, pierce leather, pull thread through, and pierce where you want the second stitch.

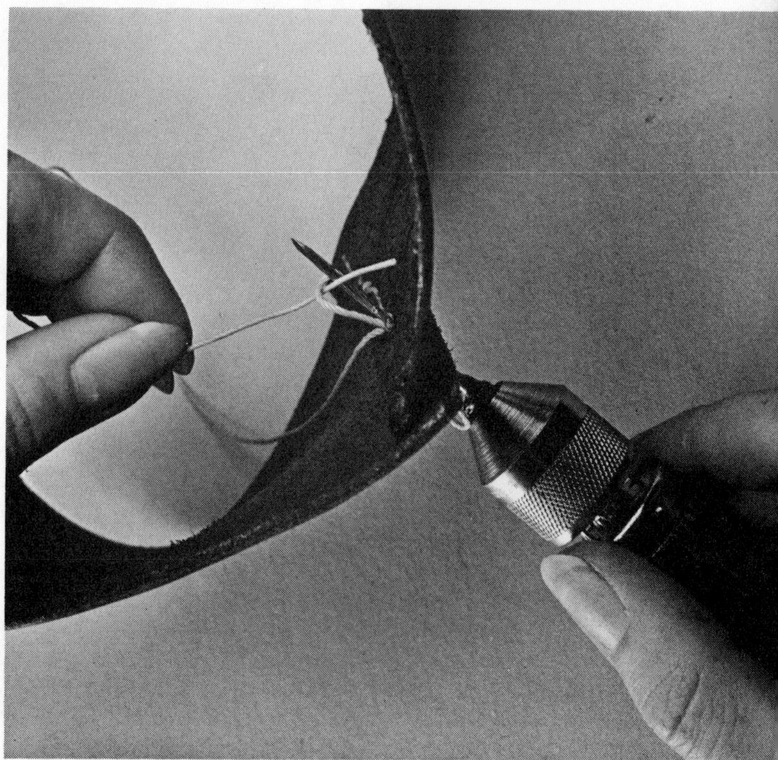

AFTER PIERCING leather for second stitch, pull needle out slightly and pull thread end through loop.

18) and linen or cotton-wrapped polyester thread are needed. (A special triangular pointed sewing machine needle will be helpful, as will a roller foot.)

Long stitches (7 to 10 per inch) are recommended, depending on the thickness of the leather. (The thinner the leather, the shorter the stitch can be.) In determining the length of the stitch remember that the needle actually punches a hole in the leather, and the more perforated by holes the leather becomes, the weaker the seam will be. (On other fabrics the needle just goes in between the woven threads.) Before sewing a project, always test the stitch and its tension on a piece of scrap.

To prevent the leather from stretching or binding, help it through the machine's feed and go slowly. Operate the machine by hand to avoid breaking the needle or thread when sewing three or more thicknesses or where two seams meet. A piece of heavy paper beneath the leather will prevent scars in the surface from the feed dog.

Finish seams by tying the ends of the thread together or turning the leather around and sewing back along the seam for a short distance. Do not backstitch by using the machine's reverse lever.

Leather that is heavier than about 3 or 4 ounces will probably have to be sewn by hand or an industrial sewing machine. If you do decide to buy an industrial sewing machine, look around for a used one, for new models are rather expensive. Shoe repair shops, sewing machine stores, want ads, and even commercial garment manufacturers are likely sources.

DRY-BONDING type contact cement must be applied to both surfaces and allowed to become tacky dry.

Bonding and Laminating

Lacing, riveting, and sewing are fine for holding edges of leather together, but when the surfaces of two or more pieces must be laminated against each other contact, rubber, or special leather cement is used. Of the many kinds and brands of cement on the market, the best one for leatherwork is a strong, all-purpose, dry-bonding contact cement or a cement made especially for leatherwork. Rubber cement is fine for lighter gluing jobs, but it is inadequate where strength is an essential factor. Another rule: don't use a glue or cement that becomes hard and brittle when it dries, since these crack and weaken as the leather bends and flexes.

Application of different brands of contact and leather adhesives vary somewhat (always follow the manufacturer's instructions), but generally a thin coat of the cement is applied to both surfaces and allowed to become tacky before the pieces of leather are put together. The only thing to remember is that a bond is created as soon as the pieces touch each other, and so alignment must be accurate the first time because the pieces can't always be adjusted. You can cut corners some by not waiting as long for the cement to dry before putting the pieces together. If you do this, watch that the pieces don't curl; press them together firmly until the cement is dry, then check again after 10 minutes or so.

Rubber cement is applied much like contact cement; because it is not as strong, the leather can be pulled apart easily if you make a mistake.

If you are cementing the smooth grain side of a piece of leather rough it up first with coarse sandpaper for best success.

Whatever kind of adhesive you use, first try it out on pieces of scrap to see if it will mar the color of the leather. Apply it sparingly at first so that it won't soak through and discolor the other side of the leather.

Excess cement can usually be cleaned up by just rubbing it into a ball. Cement won't, however, clean up from sueded leather.

Findings and Fastenings

Special hardware that you might be using as closures and reinforcing are snaps, harness buttons, grommets, and eyelets.

Snaps. Two-part snaps consist of two, two-piece parts: a socket and cap assembly, and a stud and post assembly. To install snaps, a special setting die and anvil that come as a kit are needed.

The socket and cap assembly go on the top piece of leather, the stud and post go on the bottom piece.

First punch a hole in both pieces of leather where you want them to snap together. (Each hole should be just large enough for the socket or post to fit through.)

Set the socket and cap assembly first as shown in the drawing. Push the socket through the hole in the top piece of leather from the underside and press the cap in place over it on the outside. Fit

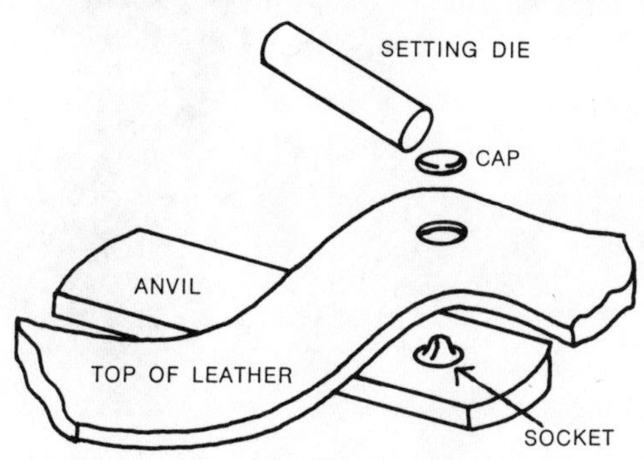

FIT SOCKET through hole with cap over it, then with socket on anvil, use setting die and hammer together.

the socket over one of the small pegs on the anvil, then place the concave end of the setting die (usually a round metal bar) on the cap and tap it with a hammer to lock the cap and socket together.

Set the stud and post in the bottom piece of leather as you did the socket and cap as illustrated in the drawing. Insert the post through the hole from the underside. Press the stud over the post and set the post over one of the pegs in the anvil. Now put the hollow end of the setting die over the stud and tap with a hammer.

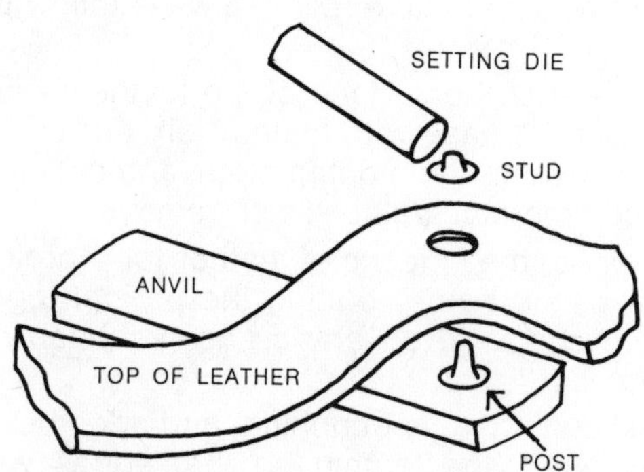

POST AND STUD go together through hole as did cap and socket. Use setting die and anvil to set them.

Harness buttons. For buttoning pieces of thick leather together, a harness button can be used. It is just a brass post that is screwed into the bottom piece of leather and pushed through a hole in the top piece. To install one, first punch a hole in the piece of leather where you want the button to go. Insert the screw through the hole and screw the button onto the threaded end from the frontside of the piece of leather as shown in the drawing. Punch another hole in the other piece of leather for the button to go through. To make buttoning and unbuttoning easier, cut a ½-inch-long slit in the buttonhole.

Eyelets and grommets. Lacing holes can be reinforced with eyelets or grommets so that lace can

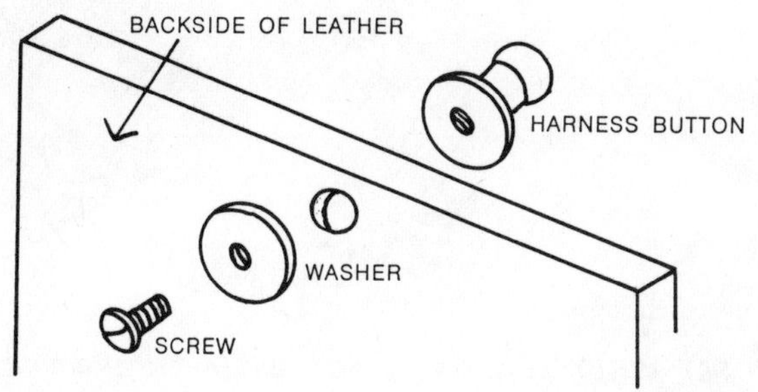

FIT SCREW through washer and then hole from backside of leather, then screw into the button.

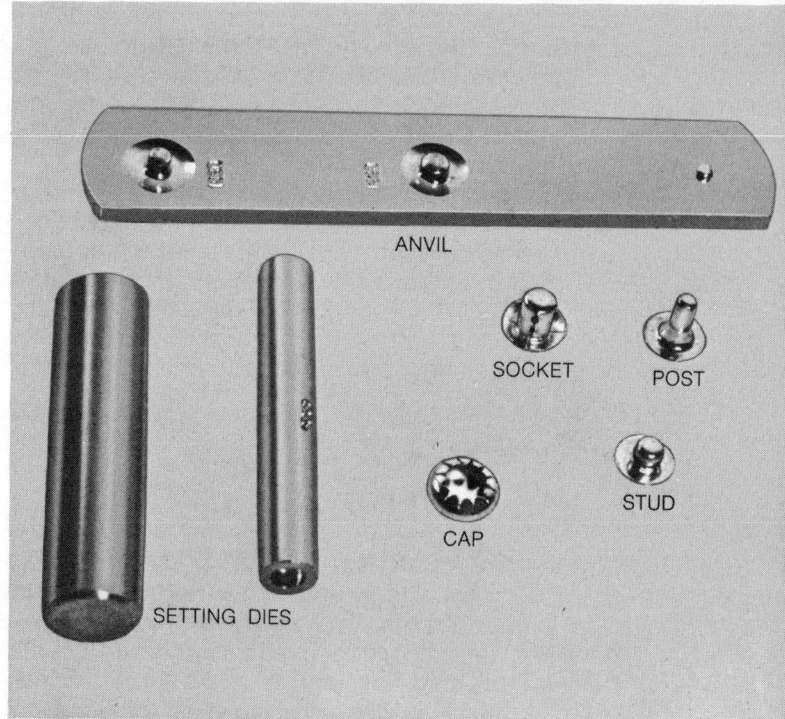

SNAP SETTING KIT includes anvil and setting dies; snaps consist of cap and socket, stud and post.

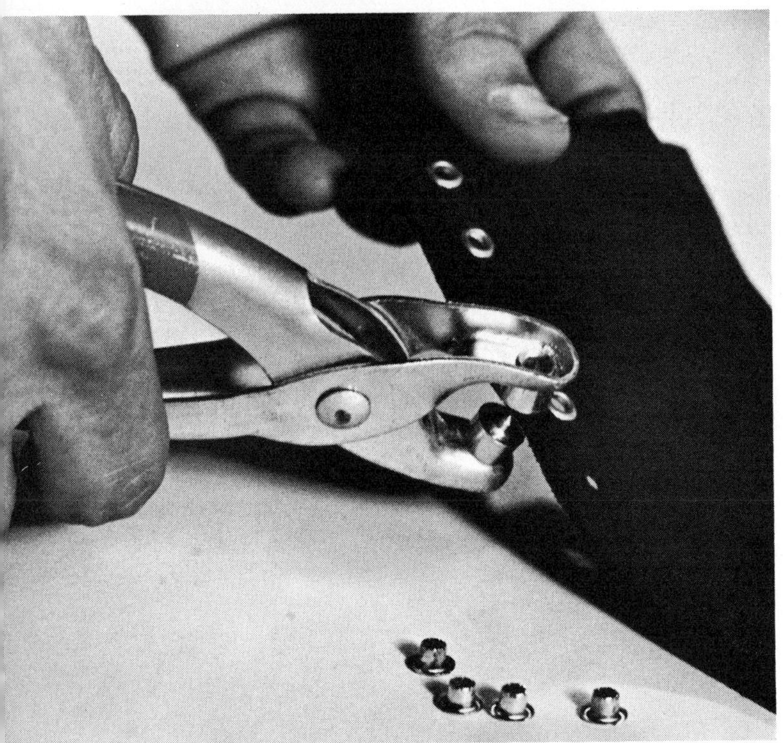

TO SET AN EYELET, insert it into a hole in leather and then squeeze it flat with a plier-like eyelet tool.

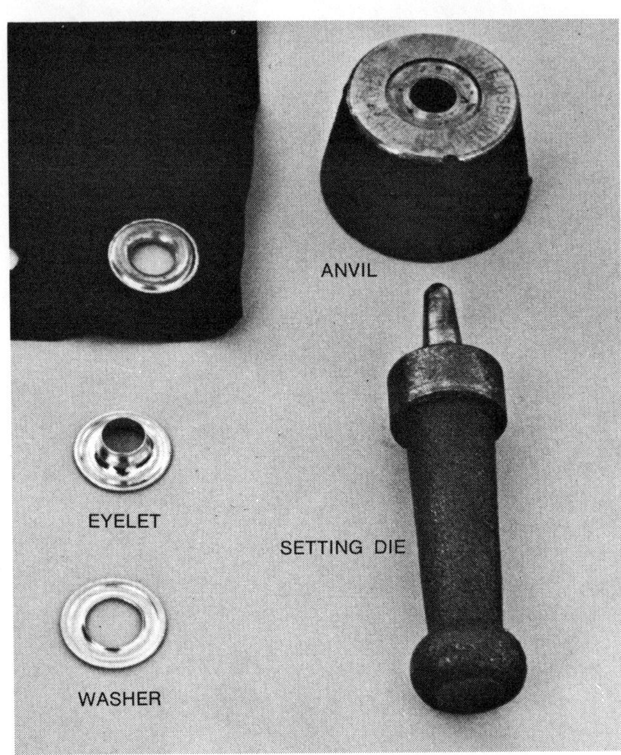

GROMMETS consist of a washer and eyelet. To set one you'll need a kit containing anvil and setting die.

be drawn through them more easily. Grommets or eyelets are primarily used when a project is laced and unlaced to open or close it. Eyelets are easier to set than grommets, but grommets have a nicer appearance and provide more strength.

To set an eyelet, punch a hole in the leather, insert the eyelet and squeeze it flat with a special eyelet plier. Eyelets and an eyelet plier are usually sold together in a package.

Grommets consist of two parts: an eyelet and a washer. A grommet setting kit is used to install one in the leather. Punch a hole in the leather and then insert the eyelet through it from the top side of the leather. Place the grommet, eyelet side down, on the anvil, and place the washer over the tube. Now place the setting die over the tube and hit the end with a hammer to squash it flat.

DYEING LEATHER

Chrome-tanned and sueded leather (see page 8) are usually dyed to various colors at the tannery. Oak-tanned leather and yellow latigo cowhide, however, are not tannery dyed and come in a neutral tan and yellow respectively. If you want leather in a color that isn't stocked at the store you shop at, just get yellow latigo or oak-tanned leather and dye it to the color you want at home. Chrome-tanned, sueded, and other specially finished leathers are not receptive to home dye jobs, and you should be very careful about trying to dye them yourself, since it may streak or mar the finish.

Three kinds of coloring agents, produced especially for leather, are leather dye, "natural" or "antique" finish, and a special leather paint. Felt pens, acrylic paints, bleach, and anything else that leaves a stain can be used for less traditional coloring effects. Though they may fade in sunlight or rub off with wear, you can at least experiment with them.

Coloring agents made especially for leather can be applied in various ways and combinations to achieve different effects. But whichever kind you use, and however you apply it, always follow these rules:

- Be sure that the surface of the leather is clean. Remove any grease with mineral oil, dirt and dust with warm water and a damp cloth, and old finishes with a commercial leather-finish remover.
- Dye or stain all pieces of leather for a project at the same time before putting the project together to insure complete coverage and reasonably uniform color.
- Do all cutting, hole punching, and edge beveling before dyeing the leather so that edges will be colored at the same time surfaces are.
- *Always* practice on pieces of scrap before tackling your project in order to find out how much dye

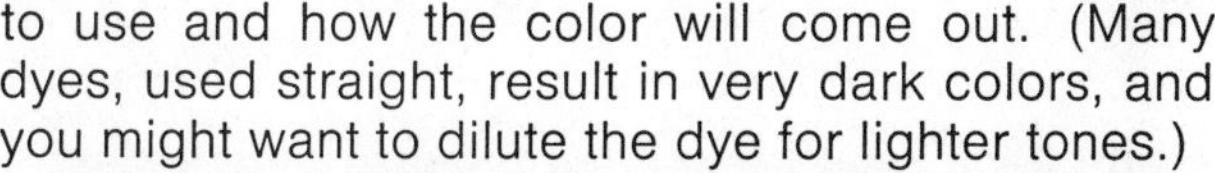

DYED SAMPLES clockwise from top: lines from natural blemishes in hide; streaked, daubed, lightly rubbed.

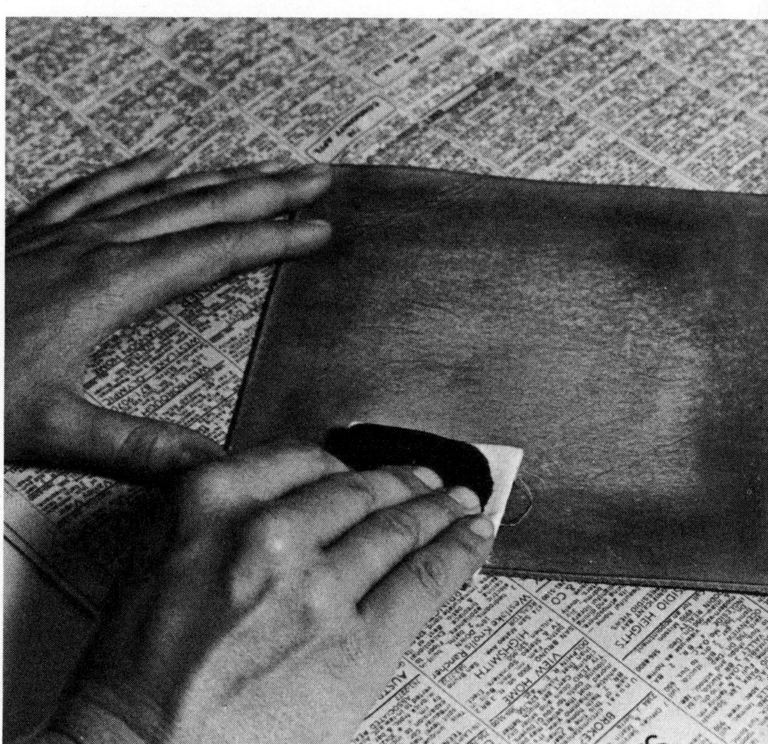

APPLY DYE with a clean cloth. Graduated tones are created by rubbing edges with more dye than center.

to use and how the color will come out. (Many dyes, used straight, result in very dark colors, and you might want to dilute the dye for lighter tones.)

- Follow manufacturer's instructions for using dye, antique or natural finish, and special leather paint. Allow plenty of time for drying.
- Remember that leather isn't a factory-perfect product, and a piece usually won't absorb the same amount of color uniformly. Since this is natural, the resulting slightly uneven color often enhances the leather's appearance.

Dyes

Basically, a dye consists of a coloring agent carried in a mineral oil, alcohol, or water base solution that soaks into the leather and then evaporates, leaving the color right in the fibers. Various browns, cordovans, yellows, blues, reds, greens, just about any other color you might want are all available, but they work best if you start with yellow latigo or neutral tan-colored oak-tanned leather rather than leather that has already been dyed or specially finished at the tannery.

Applying dye. The most straightforward method of dyeing leather is to wipe the dye on with a cloth, or piece of lamb's wool, over the entire piece of leather. (A pipe cleaner or small paint brush is helpful for small areas, touch ups, and dyeing tooled or stamped designs.)

A truly even tone of color is practically impossible, since some areas of a piece of leather will absorb more dye than others. But the objectionable "brush stroke" effect resulting from uneven application can be eliminated.

Dip the applicator in the dye and blot out all excess dye that otherwise would be absorbed immediately in the first area you touch. Now, using a circular and back and forth motion, rub the applicator over the surface of the leather as evenly as possible. Work from one end of the piece to the other, taking care not to miss spots or to stay longer in one area than another. When the applicator becomes dry, replenish it quickly with more dye and continue. (Remember always to blot excess dye out of the applicator.)

After the dye has dried, some type of protective sealer or finish is usually applied to prevent water spotting and fading and to give the surface a smooth, glossy feel. These finishes include "antique" or natural finishes and other commercial finishes (see page 33).

Light colors and special effects. Using dye straight out of the bottle usually produces a very deep color. Lighter tones and best control of streaking are gained by diluting the dye with its base solution. (Ask the sales person when you purchase the dye or look on the label to find out if the dye has a water, solvent, or oil base.)

Diluting reduces the amount of color agent in the solution so that less actual color is absorbed by the leather with each application of dye. This gives you more time for spreading the dye on evenly, and, through successive applications, the color can be built up gradually to the desired shade, while streaks left by the previous coat are covered.

Don't be afraid to dilute the dye with two or even three times the amount of water or solvent per volume of dye. If the solution turns out too weak, more coats can be applied to the leather, or the mixture can be strengthened by adding dye to it.

• *Gradual toning* creates an attractive highlighting effect. This can be done two ways. One is to make successive applications of diluted dye to areas you want darkest. The other method is to use a folded cloth from which all excess dye has been squeezed out, and softly rub light areas and increase pressure on the applicator as you move into areas you want dark.

• *Streaked effects* are achieved by brushing the dye on lightly with a cloth so that the high areas of the surface receive more dye than lower ones.

• *Blotting dye* onto leather produces a mellow, aged appearance or a unique tie-dyed effect, depending on the amount of dye used and how much space is left between the blotches.

• *Batiking* is an interesting technique used to decorate the projects on pages 50 and 68. Apply melted wax to the surface of the leather where you don't want color. (Or cover the whole surface, then partially crack the dried wax by bending the leather.) After you have let the wax dry, dip the leather into dye or apply it with a sponge. The leather will be colored wherever there is no wax. After the dye has dried completely, the wax can be removed by melting it with a hot iron. Place several layers of newspaper between the leather and iron to absorb the wax. Do not batik sueded leather.

Antique and Natural Finishes

"Antique" or "natural" finish preparations differ from dyes in that, rather than staining the actual fibers of the leather, they darken the tone of the surface, emphasizing the natural grain and texture of the leather, then polish to a deep lustre.

Some brands of finish have a sealer mixed in that prevents the color from rubbing off; others don't. So if you use antique or natural finish on articles that will come into contact with clothing or other objects that could be stained, be sure either to choose a brand that does contain a sealer or to apply a protective finish (see page 33).

WOOLSKIN is used to apply a thick, even coat of antique or natural finish over the surface of a piece of leather.

Antique and natural finishes have a paste or cream-like consistency. Though easy to apply, they require a method quite different from that of dye.

Using a sponge or piece of lamb's wool, spread the finish liberally and evenly onto the leather, leaving a thick coat over the entire surface. Let it soak in for a while, then wipe it off with a clean cloth.

The longer you wait before wiping the finish off, the darker the tone of the leather will become. As soon as the finish begins to dry, however (you'll know it's dry when it no longer has a glossy sheen), it must be wiped off. If allowed to remain longer, the finish will be hard to remove and will create streaks. To get a darker tone (if you find you have cleaned off the finish too soon), repeat the process as many times as necessary, until it is the tone you want.

After wiping off the finish, polish the leather with a clean cloth to produce a lustrous shine.

Finish that has dried and won't clean up can be removed with a damp cloth or another application. For light coloring, dilute the finish as you would a dye (above, left) or let it sit on the leather only for a few minutes, then quickly wipe it off.

Leather Paint

Some leather suppliers offer a paint-like coloring that is applied to the surface of the leather with a brush for bright highlights of color, often in conjunction with tooled and stamped designs. The paint, available in a full spectrum of colors, remains flexible and won't chip off or flake.

If you use leather paint as well as a dye, apply the paint only after dyeing has been completed. Finishes (both protective and colored) may mar or streak the paint.

DECORATING LEATHER

Decoration is one aspect of leatherworking about which craftsmen often disagree. Some feel that it detracts from the natural beauty of the leather; others highlight their work with decorative touches but are careful not to emphasize it above the design of the project and kind of leather used; and other craftsmen see leather as a perfect material for artistic self-expression and use decoration as the main feature of their work. You should always feel free to decorate your work as much or as little as you like.

Craftsmen are inventive in finding new ways of decorating leather. But the most frequently used methods are "modeling," "stamping," and burning. Designs and patterns are burned into leather by tracing the hot tip of a soldering iron or wood burning iron over the surface. Modeling and stamping both involve pressing the surface down to create designs from raised and lowered areas.

Modeling

Modeling consists of creating a design or pattern on dampened leather by pressing down the surface with the tip of a "modeling tool." Tools come with many different tips for various modeling styles. For general modeling, use a tool with a point at one end for tracing lines and a spoon-shaped tip at the other for pressing down larger areas of the surface.

A "swivel knife" is used in modeling to cut lines into the leather's surface. As you pull the knife through the leather, applying pressure with the forefinger, the blade is turned between the third finger and thumb. The resulting cut emphasizes outlines of decorations. By pressing down the sides of the cut with the spoon-shaped end of the modeling tool, you can create relief designs.

To model a piece of leather, first trace the design lightly in pencil onto the surface of the leather. Mistakes can be erased. Patterns too complicated to draw freehand onto the leather can be traced on a piece of paper which is then taped to the leather.

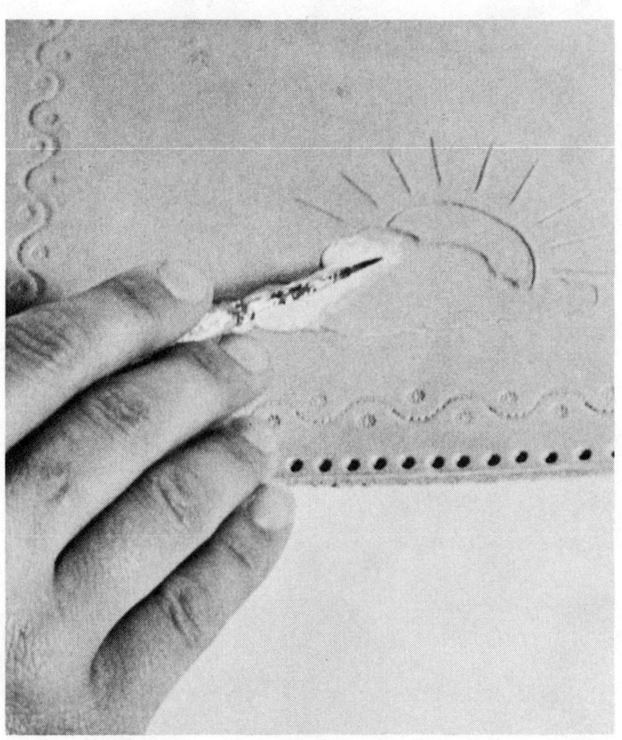

SPECIAL LEATHER PAINT, applied with a small paint brush, highlights stamped and modeled designs.

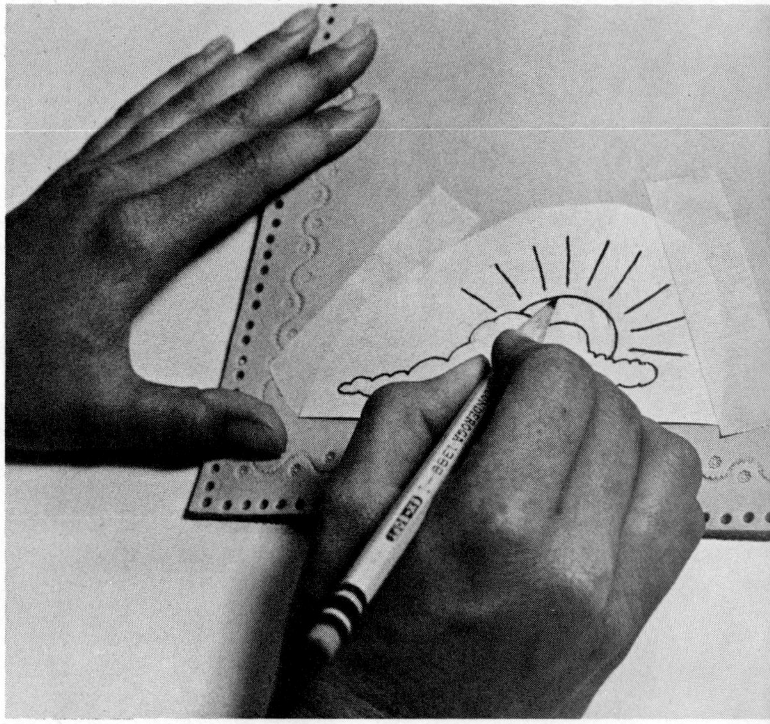

TO MODEL leather, first trace the design onto the surface. Paper pattern is used for intricate designs.

Use a pencil to go over the outline of the design, and press it onto the leather. After removing the paper, model the leather as you normally would.

Dry leather is too stiff to model easily. Wet leather is more workable and dries permanently to the shape or design you give it. So, before starting, moisten the backside of the leather until the front side is evenly damp, not dampening it so much that water squeezes out when it is pressed.

Stamping

Like modeling, stamping is a way of pressing a design into the surface of the leather, but instead of using a modeling tool and swivel knife which create the effect of a relief drawing, metal stamping dies that have a design cast into the end are driven with a hammer straight down against the surface of the leather to leave an impression. (Stamping dies don't need to be hit very hard. They should be tested first on scraps.)

Stamping works best if a hard flat surface is placed beneath the leather. Always moisten the leather before stamping as described for modeling.

Stamping dies come in an almost infinite variety of designs. The skill and creativity of using them lies in arranging one or more in an overall decorative pattern. Using only 2 or 3 different stamping dies in a single decoration is best, since more than that often create an unsatisfactory confusion rather than the desired good-looking result. Stamping dies that have a simple, abstract pattern are much more versatile than those with a more definitive figure.

You may want to try making your own stamping dies out of 16 or 20 penny nails. First cut the point of the nail off with a hack saw, then file the head flat and smooth. Using small triangular, round, and half-round files, cut the design you want into the surface of the nail's head.

LEATHER CARE

Leather can be preserved almost indefinitely if it is properly taken care of. A wide variety of different kinds and brands of commercial leather conditioners, cleaners, and protective finishes are on the

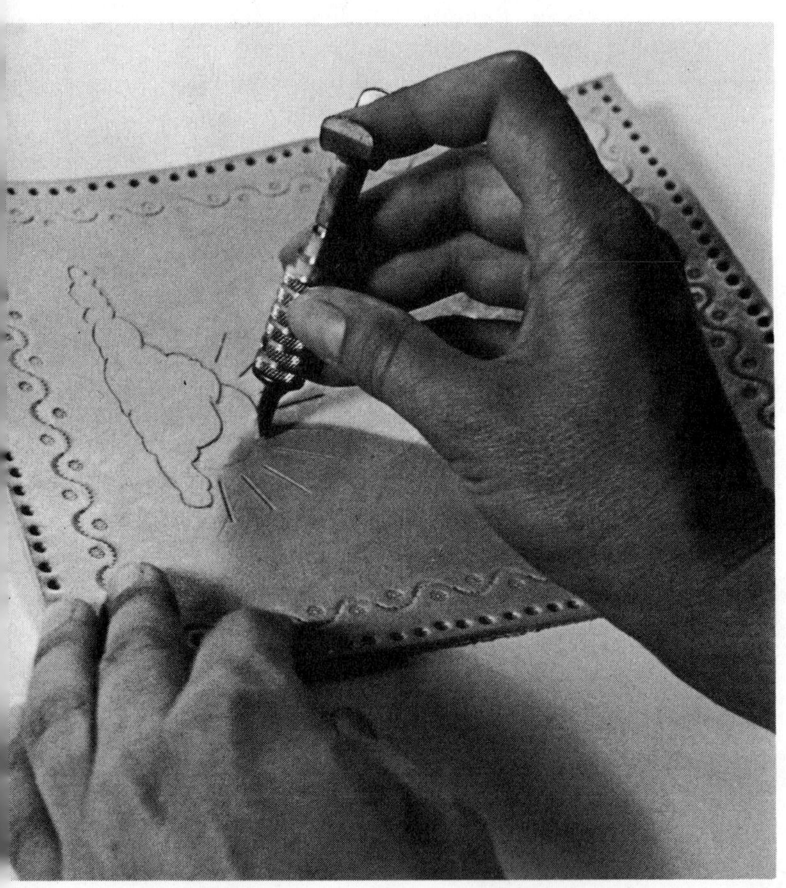

SWIVEL KNIFE cuts lines in the surface of leather. Apply pressure with forefinger, turn blade between other fingers.

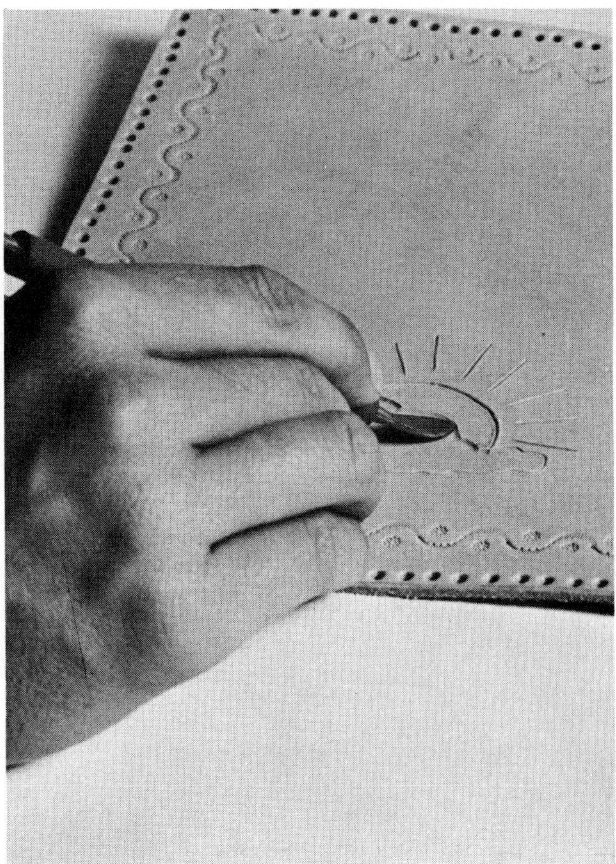

USE THE SPOON-SHAPED tip of a modeling tool to bevel swivel knife cuts and achieve relief designs.

market, usually in the form of a paste, cream, or oil. Some of them claim to condition, clean, and protect leather all in one step. (Unless specifically recommended by the manufacturer, oils, creams, and pastes are not generally used on sueded leather.)

Conditioners and Finishes

What a conditioner does is replenish the oils of leather lost because of moisture, sun, and wear. These oils are what keep the leather soft, protect it from moisture, and prevent cracking and drying out.

Neat's-foot oil, or silicone oil, the base of many leather conditioners, is excellent for most kinds of leather. Simply work it into the surface of the leather with a cloth, then wipe it off. Apply a conditioner as often as necessary to keep the leather soft, hide scratches, and protect the surface from cracking.

Commercial finishes are applied to leather as a top-dressing to protect against water spotting, fading, and staining. (Conditioners only prevent moisture from drying out, resulting in stiffening of the leather.)

Cleaners

Since leather is the skin of an animal, it can be cleaned with warm water and mild soap, just like your own. Be sure, though, to rinse out the soap.

Water usually causes leather to stiffen and crack unless natural oils that get washed out are replenished with a conditioner after the bath. Saddle soap is a fairly standard leather cleaner, but again, too many applications without the use of a conditioner afterwards will dry and crack the leather.

Split leather and suedes are cleaned by brushing the nap with fine-grit sandpaper or a wire brush. This both removes dirt and refurbishes the nap. Never use a commercial leather cleaner or conditioner on split or sueded leather unless specifically recommended by the manufacturer.

Spots and stains can be cleaned from split and sueded leather with some commercial spot removers, but always try them out first on an area that won't show, to be sure that they won't leave a ring or damage the color of the leather.

If you are uncertain about cleaning any leather article yourself, take it to a commercial dry cleaner who is prepared to handle leather goods.

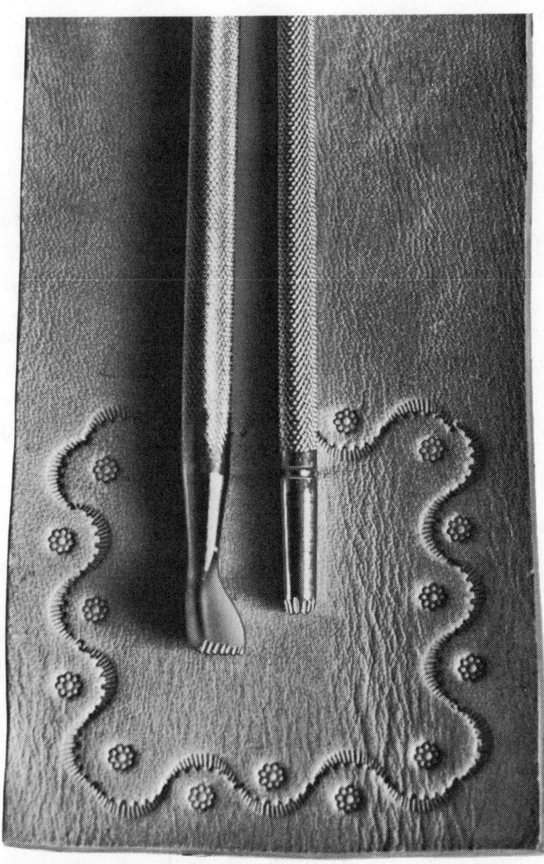

ONLY TWO stamping dies with abstract designs can be used to decorate leather with a simple pattern.

STAMPING DIES can be made at home by filing and drilling designs into the heads of large nails.

THINGS TO MAKE WITH LEATHER

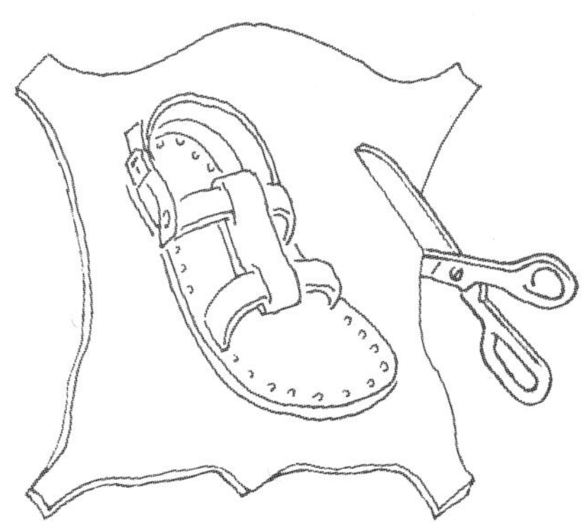

In the three previous chapters, leather and leatherworking tools and techniques have been described. The section that follows presents a wide variety of specific projects along with instructions telling how to make them. A list of the tools and leather you'll need for each project also appears in the instructions.

The leatherworking tools are described in detail on pages 12-19. You should always try tools out on scraps of leather before starting your project, especially if you are new to leatherworking.

In case the type of leather that the project was made from is not available to you, alternatives are suggested. The terms used to describe the different kinds of leather are explained on pages 6-11.

Which Project First?

The projects are not arranged in a special order that you must follow when making them. They do, however, vary in the amount of time required to make them, the tools you need, and the techniques involved.

If you are careful and read the instructions thoroughly before starting, you should have no major difficulty making a billfold, hat, purse, or similar project first.

You might, however, prefer to gain some experience at leatherwork by beginning with an easier project. If so, a checkbook cover (page 44), a belt (page 36), or the leather box (page 69) are fairly simple, and each will familiarize you with one or more of the basic techniques used on larger projects.

Decorating and Dyeing Projects

Some of the projects described have been dyed and/or decorated before being assembled. Decorating and dyeing leather are always optional and purely a matter of personal taste, and you can do so whether the project shown was or not.

If you do decide to decorate or dye the leather, just remember that oak-and oil-tanned cowhide are best for both decorating and dyeing. See pages 28-32 for dyeing and decorating techniques.

A Note About Patterns

Before you start many projects, it is a good idea to make a paper pattern for each of the parts of the project. A pattern will assist in marking and cutting the leather accurately, and you can also take it along when you shop for leather to assure getting enough with as few leftover scraps as necessary.

For many of the projects, a drawing of the pieces of leather you'll need to cut is provided, and all you have to do is transfer the measurements onto paper and cut them out. To use the pattern, just lay the pattern down onto the leather and trace around its outlines in pencil or chalk.

Leather Hang-up

THE LEATHER WORKS

KIRIGAMI PAPER CUTTING techniques were used to make this basket that might hold a candle, fishbowl, or potted plant.

This hanging basket is made out of a 9-inch-wide circle of 8-9 ounce latigo cowhide, but chrome-tanned cowhide could be used instead. Two thongs serve as hangers. The only tools you'll need are a utility knife, a No. 5 hole punch, and a compass.

First, cut a 9-inch-diameter circle out of heavy paper and fold it in half three times to make the pie-wedge shown in drawing. With the point of the compass on the pointed end of the pattern, draw an arc 1 inch out, then another every ½ inch, making seven lines in all. The arcs do not go all the way across the wedge but stop about ½ inch from alternate edges.

With a pair of scissors, cut along each line, stopping ½ inch from each alternate edge. Unfold the pattern, tape it to the leather surface, and mark each cut in the pattern onto the leather with a pencil. Now cut leather along each line with the utility knife, being careful to stop and start each cut where lines begin and end. As the photograph demonstrates, cutting is easiest if you nail the center of the leather to a piece of wood, push the knife through the leather at the beginning of a line, and rotate the leather. Cut the center of the circle out completely—the finished basket will hang from this disc.

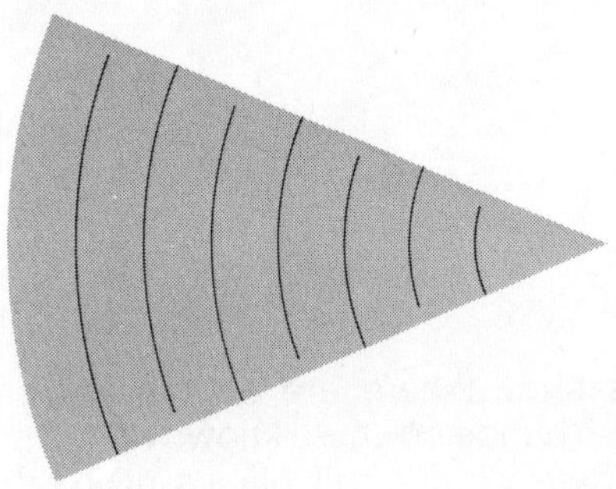

Punch four equally spaced holes along edges and another in the center of the disc. Punch four holes in the outer ring of basket: one in the center of each cut (see photograph). If you wish, dye the leather and thongs. (See pages 28-32.)

To hang the basket, cut two thongs to twice the length you want the basket to hang and tie a knot in one end of each thong. Thread the end of one thong up through a hole in basket ring, in and out two adjacent holes in center ring, then back down through hole in the strap. Knot the end of the thong. Repeat with the second thong. Hang the entire basket from a short thong knotted through the hole in center of the disc.

NAIL CENTER OF LEATHER to a piece of wood, push the knife through at the start of a line, and then rotate the leather.

THE LEATHER WORKS

BELTS can have many styles. Here is a belt with a conventional buckle that requires a keeper (buckles also come in styles not requiring a keeper), another that uses two brass rings, and a third incorporating one ring.

Three Belts

The belts shown here are all made from single strips of 8-9 ounce cowhide known as "belt blanks." You can buy pre-cut belt blanks at leather shops in a wide range of widths, long enough to be cut down to fit your waist, or you can cut your own with a utility knife and straight edge (see page 21) or a draw gauge (page 18). In addition to a belt blank, you'll need a buckle or rings (available at leather shops). Be sure to get one that is the same width as your belt blank. Tools include a utility knife, a No. 5 round hole punch, a No. 3 edge beveler, rivets, a hammer, and a slot punch (optional).

Conventional Buckle Belts

There are two kinds of belt buckles. The one at the top of the photograph requires a "keeper" to hold the end of the belt in place; the other type does not (see page 38). Construction of a belt with either buckle, however, is similar.

First cut the belt blank to the proper length—your waist measurement plus 9 inches—then cut one end of the belt to the shape you prefer: mitered (top belt in photograph), rounded (center belt), slanted (bottom belt), or pointed.

If you are making a belt with a buckle requiring a keeper, cut a strip of leather from scrap between ⅝ and ¾ inch wide (depending on the width of the belt) and long enough to go around two thicknesses of the belt plus an extra ½ inch for overlapping the ends.

Bevel the edges of the belt and keeper. Then, if you wish, decorate and/or dye the leather as described on pages 28-32.

Next, attach the buckle to the belt. First punch a slot for the buckle tongue in the center of the belt blank 2⅛ inches from the uncut end of belt, using a round hole punch and utility knife (see page 14) or a slot punch as shown in the photo at right. The length and width of the slot depend on the size of the buckle tongue. One that is 1 inch long and ¼ inch wide will work for most average-size belt buckles.

Slip the buckle onto the end of the belt with the buckle tongue through the slot, as in the photograph at right. The tongue should be able to move freely up and down in the slot. Fold the end of the belt under, then punch a hole through underlapped

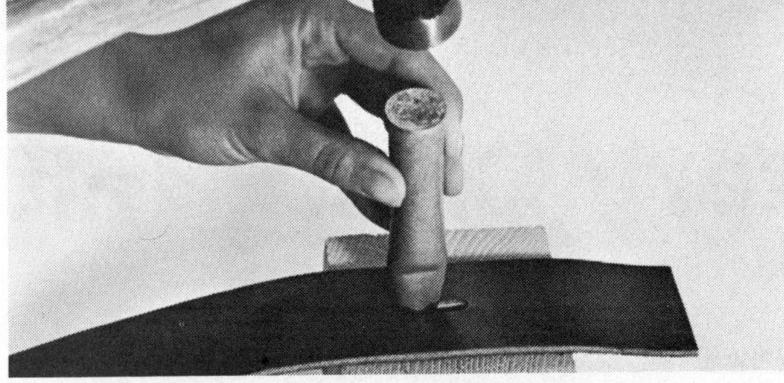

FIRST STEP in fitting a buckle is to punch a slot about 2 inches from the end of belt to insert buckle tongue.

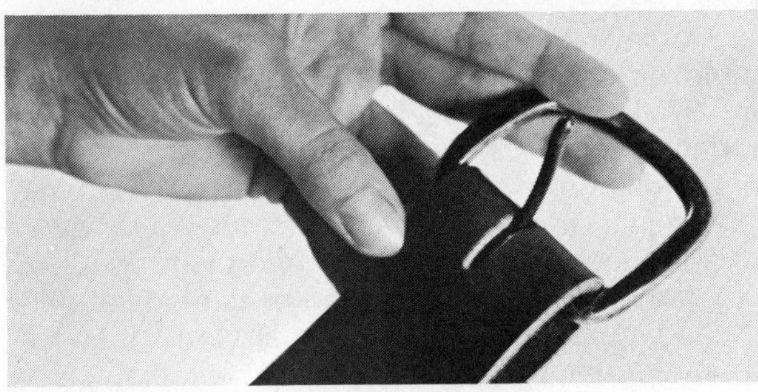

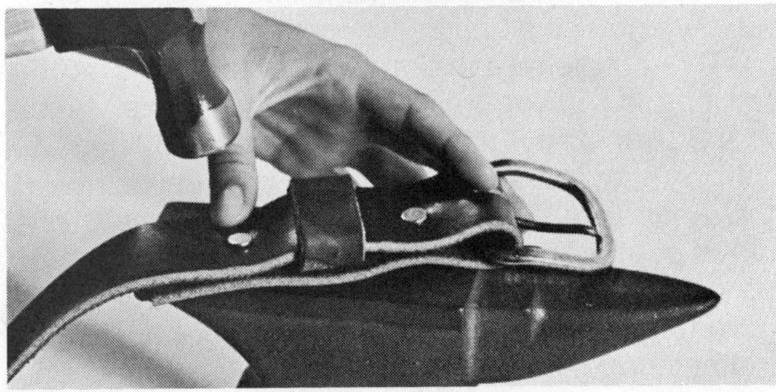

END OF THE BELT goes around the buckle, with the buckle tongue through the slot. The underlapped end is then riveted.

end of belt and belt body close to the buckle. Rivet the end of belt to the body as described on page 21. Some belts have two rivets here for decoration and extra strength.

If the buckle requires a keeper, lap the ends of the narrow strip of leather over each other to form a loop. After punching a hole in each end, rivet them together. Slide the keeper onto the belt, bringing it up close to the rivets holding the buckle. Lap the unriveted end of the underlap over the keeper, punch holes, and rivet the belt end to the belt body so that the keeper is between the two sets of rivets. (See photograph above.) If the buckle does not require a keeper, just rivet the underlapped end of the belt a second time to the body.

The final step is to punch holes in the end of the belt so that it can be buckled. Measure off the length of your waist from the end of the buckle tongue to the pointed end of the belt and punch a hole. Then make one or two more holes on either side of it.

Single Ring Belt

For the single ring belt, you'll need a 1½- to 1¾-inch-wide brass ring (for a belt blank 1½ inches wide). You'll also need two 1-inch-wide strips of leather: one 4 inches long, the other 7 inches long. Cut the belt blank to your waist size plus 5½ inches; leave both ends of the belt square. Bevel the edges of the pieces of leather, then dye and decorate them if you wish.

Wrap one end of the 4-inch strip around the ring and use one or two rivets to secure it. Following the dimensions in the diagram, rivet the other end of the 4-inch strip to one end of the belt. (The end of the ring should just meet the end of the belt.) Attach the 7-inch-long strip to the other end of the belt with two rivets, indicated by dotted circles in the diagram. The backside (flesh side) of the strip should be facing up so that the smooth grain side will show when the belt is fastened.

The belt is secured with a harness button (page 27). First punch three equally spaced holes in the 7-inch strip and cut a ½-inch-long slit behind each hole. To place the harness button, try the belt on, pulling the 1-inch strip through the ring and then back over itself. Mark the position of one of the holes in the strip onto the belt, punch a hole in the belt, and screw the harness button in place, as described on page 27.

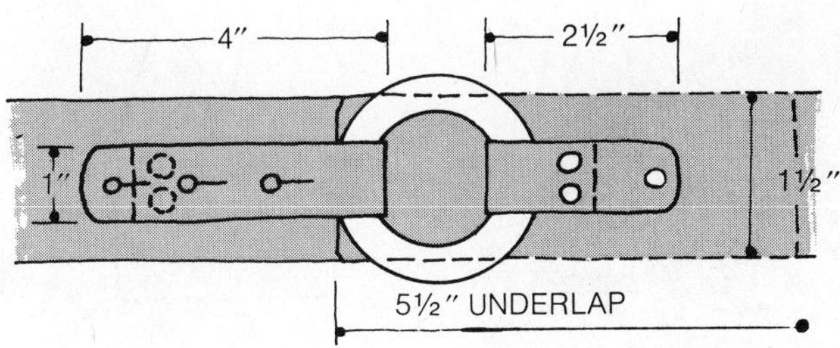

Double Ring Belt

For a double ring belt, cut the belt blank 9 inches longer than your waist. After cutting one end to the shape you want, bevel the edges and decorate or dye the leather. Wrap the uncut end of the belt around both of the rings and rivet it to the body of the belt.

The pointed end of the belt is cut off about 9 inches back, turned over, and riveted back onto the belt, flesh side up so that the smooth grain side of the end of the belt will be on the outside when the belt is fastened. Skive the ends of the pieces as described on page 17 so that the joint will be smooth.

Mystery Braid Belt

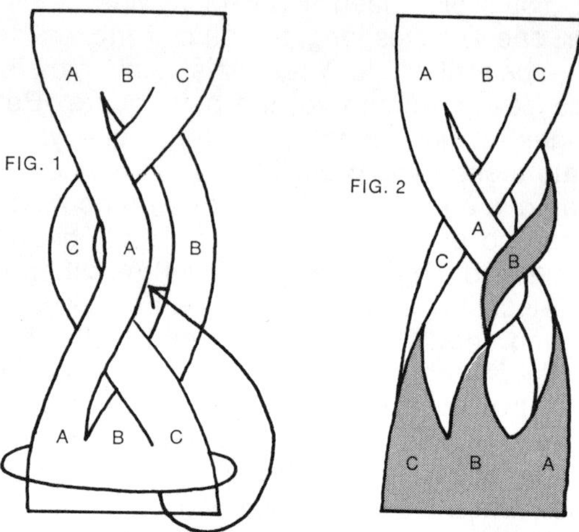

CUT THE LEATHER into three equal strips, then place strip C over B and under A. Pull the end between strips B and A.

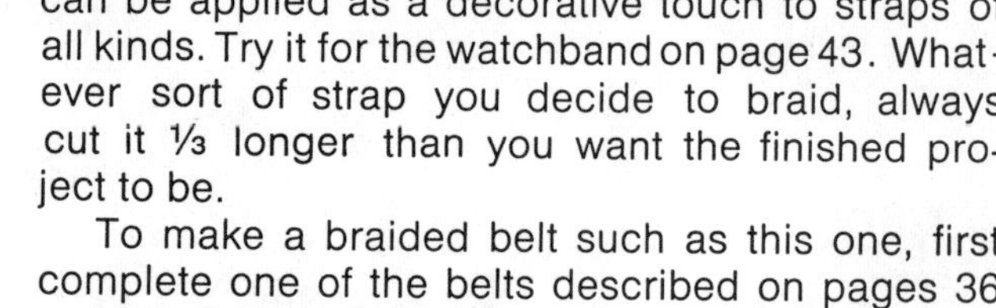

The three-strand "mystery braid" used on this belt can be applied as a decorative touch to straps of all kinds. Try it for the watchband on page 43. Whatever sort of strap you decide to braid, always cut it ⅓ longer than you want the finished project to be.

To make a braided belt such as this one, first complete one of the belts described on pages 36 and 37. Remember: cut the belt ⅓ longer than you normally would. On the finished belt, make two cuts lengthwise down the center to divide the belt into three equal strips. Start the cuts about ¾ inch away from the last buckle hole and end them about ¾ inch from the rivets holding the buckle on the belt.

Starting at either end of the belt, braid it as follows, referring to the illustrations at left: first, place strip C *over* strip B and *under* strip A. (Fig. 1.) Then pull the end of the belt between strips A and B. (Fig. 2.) This creates a tangle at the bottom end of the belt that is removed by the following steps. Place strip B *over* strip A and strip C *over* strip B. (Fig. 3.) Pull the tangled end of the belt between strips B and A as in figure 4. These steps complete one series of braiding. To finish the belt, repeat steps 1 through 4 until the belt is entirely braided. When there is no more room at the bottom of the belt for another complete series, loosen the braiding and space it out over the unbraided section.

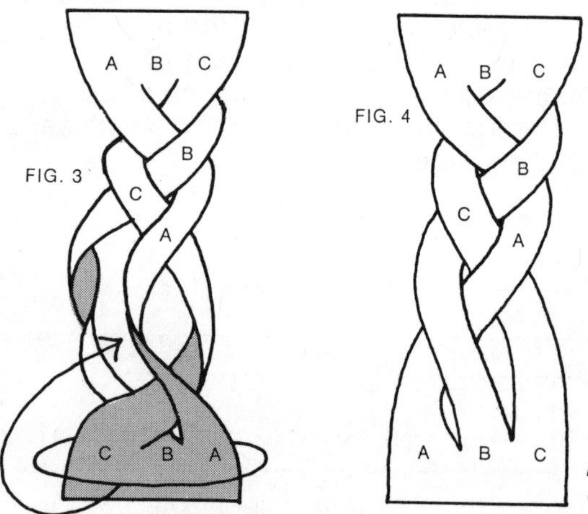

DISREGARDING TANGLE at bottom of leather, place strip B over A and under C, then pull the end between strips B and A.

THE "MYSTERY BRAID" can be applied to straps of all sorts. Here it adds a decorative touch to a belt.

MARY LOUISE CARTER

Cummerbund Belt

The inlay decoration on the front of this belt was created by cementing together the suede sides of different colored pieces of garment cowhide after the design had been cut into the outer part. To make a similar one, you'll need a small-bladed craft knife, a thonging chisel or No. 5 hole punch, a lacing needle, grommets or eyelets with the appropriate setting tool, rubber cement, and 6½ feet of lace. This belt was laced with ¼-inch-wide "garment lace" cut from sueded garment cowhide.

First cut a strip of leather for the belt's inner backing to the length of your waist measurement in the shape you want the belt to be; then cut a diamond shape from the center of the belt—producing two separate sides and a center diamond.

Using the three backing pieces as a pattern, cut three more pieces of different-colored suede for the outside of the belt. Allow an extra ½ inch along the sides of the two side pieces for folding under. The two diamonds should be the same size.

Enlarge the design (or use one of your own) and trace it onto the outer diamond in pencil. Then use the small-bladed craft knife to cut out the darkened areas in the pattern drawing. Cement the outer diamond onto the inner one.

The inner and outer side sections are laminated together in the same way the diamonds were, except that you might want to put a piece of fabric stiffener in between them to give the belt extra body. Fold the edges under.

Cut corresponding holes or slits around the diamond and edges of the sides (see drawing), then lace the edges of the diamond to the sides with the whip stitch (page 23).

If you wish, cut the sides of the belt in half, then lace them back together again to achieve a pieced effect.

The ends of the belt are laced together in the back. Punch three holes along the edges of each end of the belt and apply a grommet or eyelet (see pages 27-28) to each so that lacing and unlacing the belt will be easiest.

ALYSON SMITH GONSALVES

DIAMOND on the front of this belt is a separate piece of leather, laced to the two sides of the belt.

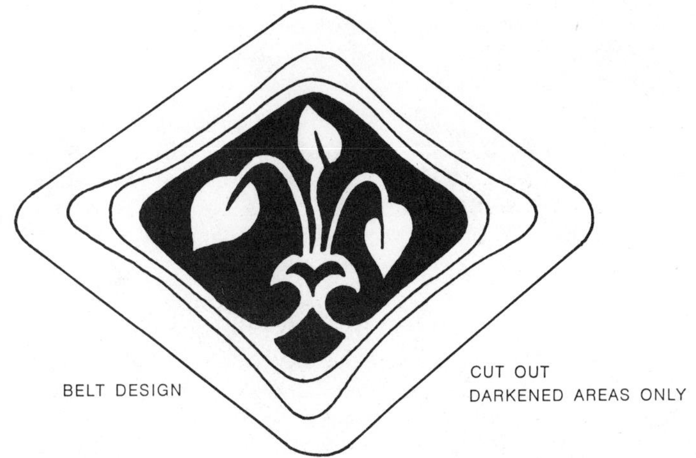

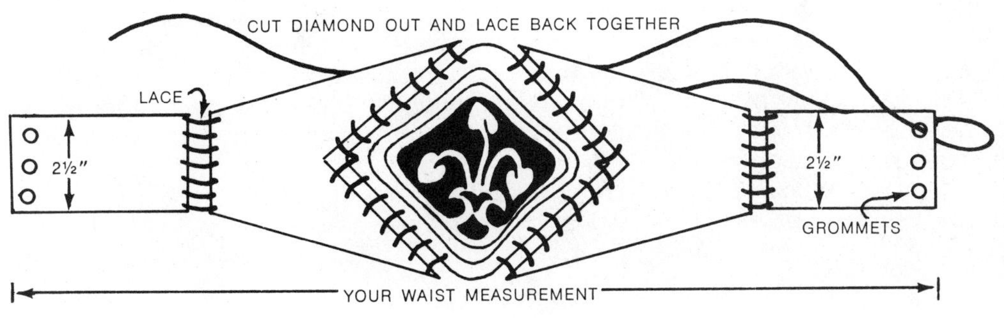

CUT A DIAMOND from the center of the belt, creating two sides and a center. After appliqueing, lace parts together.

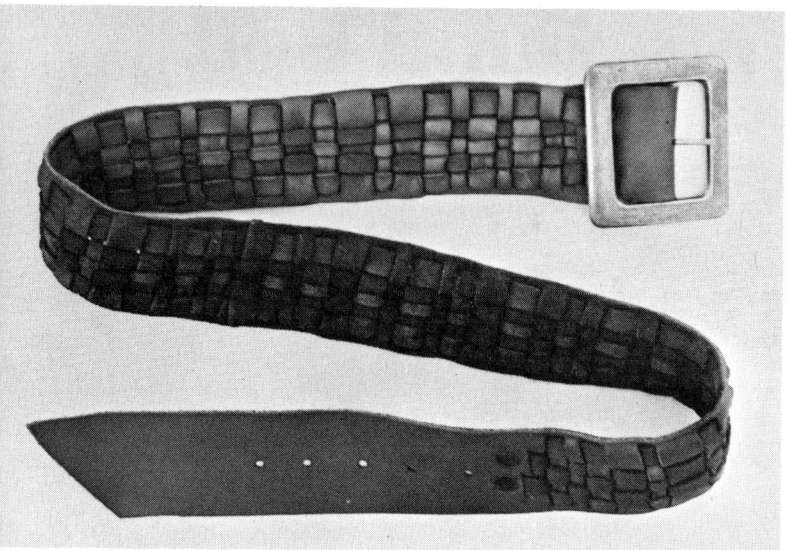

GAY STAFFORD

STRIPS OF LEATHER woven through slits cut in a belt add a unique decorative touch. Rivet strip ends beneath belt.

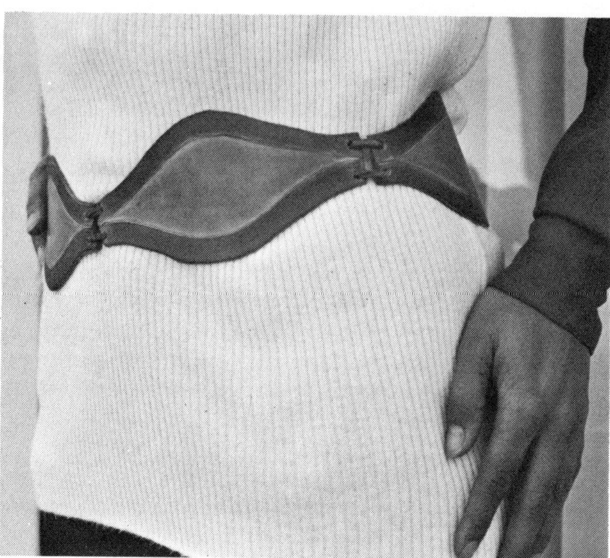

ALYSON SMITH GONSALVES

FOUR OVAL-SHAPED pieces of leather, laced together, create this belt. Cut each oval 1/4 the length of waist measurement.

Two Belts

Woman's belt (right) is made from four pieces of leather cut into oval shapes. Four ounce oak-tanned cowhide was used, but 6 ounce latigo would also work. The pieces were dyed yellow in the center, blue around the edges, and then laced together.

To make a belt like this, measure your waist and divide by four. This gives the length each section of the belt should be; its width can be whatever you want. The ovals in this belt are 6 inches long and 3 inches wide to fit a 24-inch waist.

Cut four pieces of leather to the shape you want (remember, each must be 1/4 of your waist measurement). Dye the pieces to the color you like. Then, with a No. 5 round hole punch, cut two holes in the ends of each piece and lace them together with lengths of 3/16-inch-wide thongs.

Fasten the ends of the completed belt together in the back with another piece of thong. To make lacing and unlacing the belt easier in the back, you can put a grommet or eyelet in each lacing hole, as described on page 28.

The woven belt (left) is a variation of the belts described on pages 36 and 37. It consists simply of five strips of leather woven through slits cut in the belt body. You can vary the belt by using strips of different colors. Or by making strips different widths and cutting slits at odd intervals, you can achieve a random effect. (The strips must, however, be 1/2 inch narrower than the belt when placed alongside each other.)

Start by making one of the belts described on pages 36 and 37. (The width of the belt doesn't matter, but remember that wider ones are easiest to weave.) If you use a buckle rather than rings, get one that doesn't require a keeper.

When the belt is finished, rivet the ends of the strips to the back of the belt at one end. (Strips on this belt were riveted at the same time as the buckle.)

To weave the strips, first cut three slits, each above the other and unconnected. Each slit should be just wide enough for top, middle, or bottom strip. (If you have spacing problems, cut the center slit 1/2 inch toward the center of the belt.) Now cut slits down the rest of the belt, making each slit long enough for all of the strips to be woven through. Make the last slit 3 inches from where the end of the belt goes through the buckle or rings when the belt is fastened. Now weave the strips through the slits. Start by pulling the top, middle, and bottom strips through the individual slits cut for each, then weave all five strips in and out of the slits. When you reach the last slit, two or three of the strips will be on the outside of the belt. Cut individual slits for them as you did at first and then draw all strips beneath the belt and rivet their ends to the belt.

Key Case

A key case is easy to make and will receive years of use. This one is decorated with a flat, polished stone inset into the leather. To make a key case, you'll need a razor or utility knife, a hammer, rivets, a No. 5 round drive punch (to make holes for rivets and snap), a snap, a snap setter, and a "key plate." (If you want to inset a stone in the case, you'll also need a sewing needle and 3-cord waxed nylon thread.) A heavy key case like this one can be made out of 6-7 ounce latigo or chrome-tanned cowhide. For a less bulky case, use thinner leather or even garment-type cowhide suede. You'll need a piece of leather that is about 7 by 3½ inches.

The keys are attached to the case with what is known as a "key plate," riveted in the center of the key case. The key plate in this case has six key hooks and measures about 2 inches long, but other sizes are also available.

First cut out the leather. It should be a strip that is about 2½ times the length of your key plate and 3¼ inches wide. This case is 6¼ by 3¼ inches. Cut one end of the strip so that it is slightly rounded.

Now position the key plate in the center of the strip of leather with the key hooks at the top edge of the leather. Mark the position of the rivet holes in the plate onto the leather and punch them out. Through these holes, rivet the plate onto the leather.

Fold the sides of the key case over the plate and then mark and punch holes in the ends of the leather for a snap. (Cut excess leather from the edges of the case as necessary to make them fit around the plate.) Install a snap in the holes in the ends of the case, as described on page 27.

If you wish to inset a stone in the front of the case, choose a flat, polished stone. Place it onto the backside of the case, below the key plate, then trace around it in pencil. About ¼ inch inside this outline, cut out a circle. Replace the stone on the leather inside the cut-out circle. Cut another piece of leather from scrap that is large enough to cover the stone and leave about a ¼-inch margin all the way around it. Place this piece over the stone; then sew its edge to the key case with the double running stitch.

POLISHED STONE is placed over hole in leather from inside case. Sew a piece of scrap leather over the stone to hold it.

GAY STAFFORD

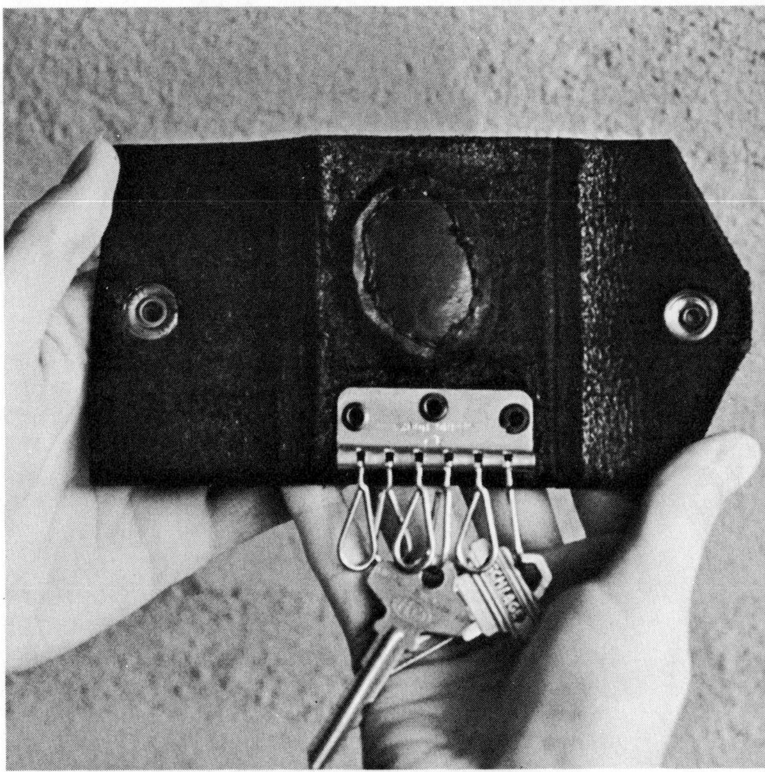

METAL KEY PLATE is riveted to the top center of the case. Piece of leather above key plate holds the stone inset.

STEVE SMITH

TWO-PART WATCHBAND can be worn as a narrow band or a wide one. The narrow and wide parts (top) are separate. To put them together, remove the watch from narrow band; thread narrow band through slots in wide band.

Watchbands

Watchbands can be made in many different styles: here are some that you might like to try.

The watchband pictured above can be worn as a wide band or a narrow one; its construction method is basic to almost all other types of watchbands.

You'll need two strips of thin leather (2 ounce latigo or oak-tanned cowhide), a small buckle, small rivets or thin lace, a knife, and a No. 1 or 2 round hole punch. Stamping dies for decorating the band and a slot punch are optional. (You do not need to bevel the edges of leather this thin.)

Make the narrow band first. It is a strip of leather as long as your wrist circumference plus 3 inches and as wide as the bars on the sides of your watch. Cut one end of the strip to a tapering point. The watchband shown here was decorated with stamped designs and then dyed brown.

The buckle you use must be the same width as the strap. Punch a slot for the buckle tongue (see page 14), 1 inch away from the square end of the strap and large enough to permit the buckle tongue to move up and down freely. (Start with a slot about 1/16 inch wide and ¼ inch long.) Fit the buckle tongue through the slot; fold the end through the buckle and under the strap. (See page 37 for further instructions on fitting buckles.) On this band the underlapped end was secured with thin lace. But if you prefer, use a small rivet. If the buckle requires a keeper as this one does, make it as described on page 36, then slide it into place near the buckle. If the keeper is not too big, tension will hold it in place on the band and you won't need to lap the end of the band over it.

Now put the pointed end of the strap through the bars of the watch. (If the leather is too thick to go through them, skive it thinner as described on page 17.) Measure the length of your wrist circumference from the end of the buckle tongue to the pointed end of the band and punch a hole for the buckle tongue. Punch another hole on both sides of it.

To make the wide part of the band, cut a strip of leather as wide as the face of the watch and as long as your wrist circumference. The ends can be rounded or left square. (Use the same leather that you used for the narrow band. Or if you prefer a heavier appearance, use a thicker leather.) Set the narrow band (with the watch on it) onto the wide one, keeping the watch face centered. On the wide band, mark the position for two slots (each as wide as the narrow band) on either side of the watch face. (See photo above.) The slots should be ½ inch apart and ½ inch from the watch.

To put the two bands together, remove the watch from the narrow band, then slip the pointed end through two of the slots. Put the watch back on the narrow band and thread the end through the other two slots.

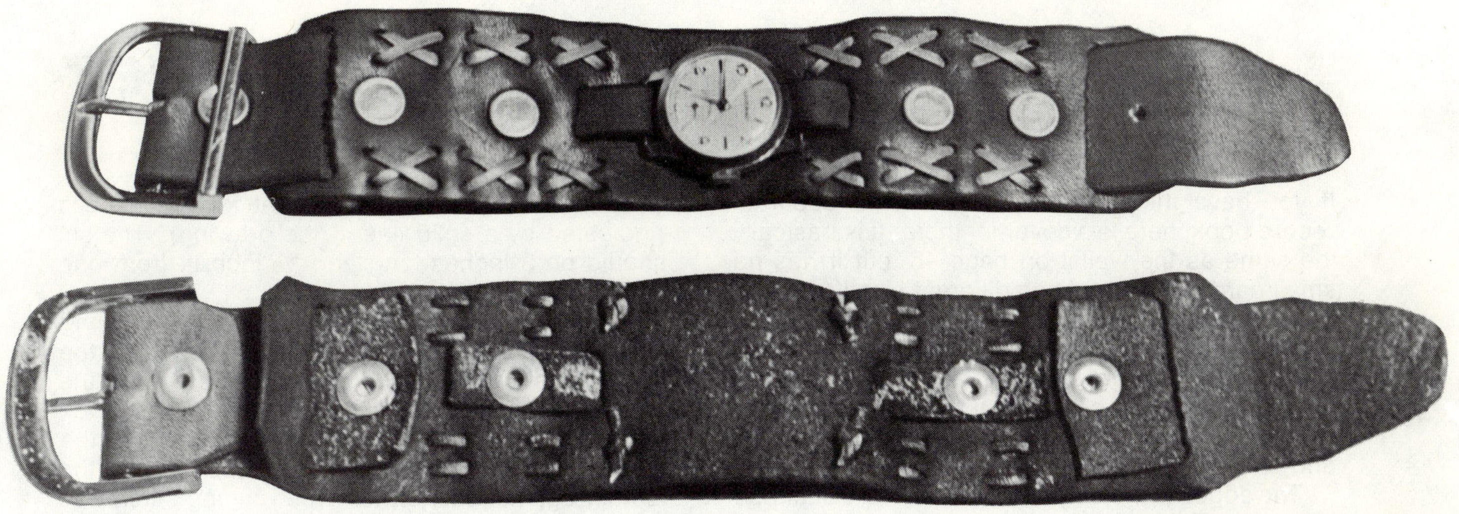

STEVE SMITH

CRISS-CROSSING LACE on this band is purely decorative. The strips of leather holding the buckle and watch are riveted to the underside of the band after being pulled through slots that were cut in the band for them.

Here are a few variations of the watchband on page 42.

The wide band (above) consists of a strip of leather as long as your wrist circumference and as wide as you like (as long as it is wider than the watch face) that has been decorated with criss-crossing 1/16-inch-wide calf lace. To lace the band, first punch two parallel sets of slits down each side of the band, then use the whip stitch to lace from one row to the other, skipping a slit on each row as you lace. When you reach the end of the band, continue lacing back in the opposite direction through the slits you had skipped.

To attach the watch to the band, thread a strip of leather (about 4 inches long) through the bars on the watch, center the watch on the wide band, and cut slots in the band for the ends of the strip to go through. Rivet the ends of the strip underneath the band.

For buckling the band, cut two strips of leather narrower than the band and about 2½ inches long. (Trim later to fit if necessary.) Attach the buckle to one of the strips (see page 37); cut the end of the other to a tapering point and punch buckle holes. Attach the strips to the band by cutting a slot in the wide band, ¾ inch in from each end, inserting the two end strips through them and riveting in place. The strips should extend 2 inches from the slots.

The braided watchband pictured at the bottom of the page is merely a strip of leather, wide enough to go through the bars on the sides of the watch, that was braided after the buckle was attached and the band put onto the watch.

To make the watchband, first cut a strip of 2 ounce leather, just wide enough to go through the bars on the watch and as long as your wrist circumference, plus ⅓ of your wrist circumference, plus another 4 inches. Attach a buckle to one end of the band and punch buckle holes in the other. Now weave the end through the bars on the watch and braid the band as described on page 38.

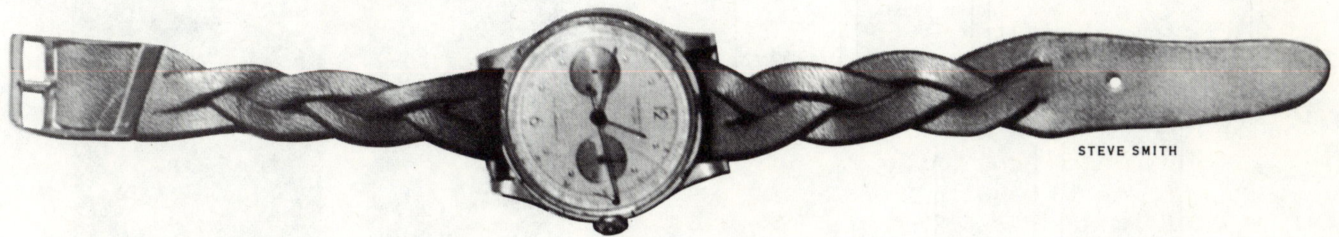

STEVE SMITH

BRAIDED WATCH BAND is just a strip of leather similar to the narrow part of the band at left. After the watch is put onto it, it is braided as described on page 38. Braid only the section on either side of the watch.

Checkbook Cover

If you have the kind of checks with a separate record book, here is a cover for them. It is basically the same as the wallet on page 45, but it has no small card pocket and has different sized pockets. Two to three ounce oak-tanned cowhide was used to make this one, but for a lighter cover you might want to use thinner leather, calfskin perhaps, or even garment-type cowhide. If you use oil- or oak-tanned cowhide, however, the cover can be tooled and carved as this one was.

The edges of the checkbook cover were stamped with two different stamping dies. A swivel knife was used to cut the outline of the sun and cloud on the front. The cuts were then beveled with a modeling tool for a relief effect. After being decorated, the cover was dyed, and leather paint was applied to the edge and front decorations.

Along with the optional decorating tools you'll need a utility knife or razor cutter, a No. 0 or 1 round hole punch (or a thonging chisel), 1/16-inch-wide calf lace, and a lacing needle. A stitch marker will help space holes punched with the round hole punch. So that the checkbook cover will fold easily, you might want to cut a V down the inside center with a V-gouge, especially if you use thick, stiff leather. If you use garment suede leather for the wallet, you might prefer to sew rather than to lace the pieces together. If so, see pages 16 and 17 for sewing tools.

Following the dimensions given in the pattern drawing, cut out the three pieces of leather: one for the body and two more for the pockets. The pockets are different widths: a wide one for the checks and a narrower one for the record book. Decorate and dye the leather if you wish as described on pages 28-32.

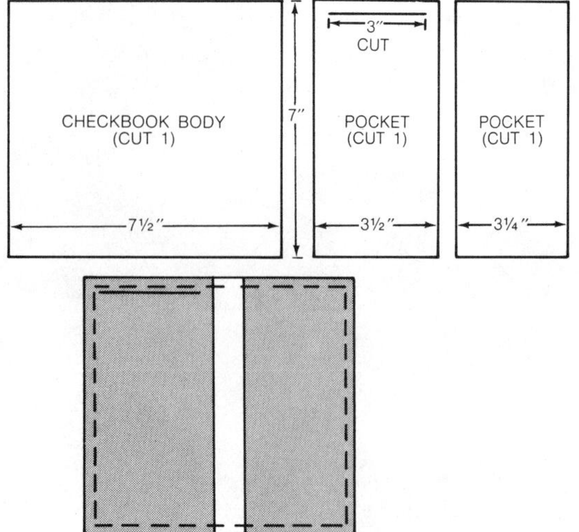

Cut a slit in the wider pocket for the checks (indicated by a solid line in the drawing). The slit should be 3 inches long and ⅝ inch in from one edge of the pocket.

To assemble the cover, punch matching lacing holes or slits all the way around the edge of the back piece and matching holes or slits around the three edges of each pocket. The holes should be ⅛ inch from the edges of all pieces. Now lace the pieces together with the flesh (back) sides of the leather against each other. The running stitch was used for this cover, but any of the other lacing stitches described on pages 22-24 can be used.

If you've used thick or stiff leather that won't bend easily, cut a V down the inside center fold line with a V-gouge.

RICHARD OSBORNE

POCKETS AND BODY of checkbook cover are laced, flesh sides of leather together. Slit in wide pocket is for checks.

RICHARD OSBORNE

MEN'S WALLET has two pockets and a card holder. It is made out of 4 ounce oak-tanned cowhide that was hand dyed dark brown. The calf lace was dyed to match. If you want a less bulky wallet, use 2-3 ounce latigo.

Men's Wallet

This sturdy men's wallet was made from 3-4 ounce oak-tanned cowhide. Thinner leather could be used instead if you want a less bulky wallet. To make one you'll need a utility knife, a No. 0 or 1 round hole punch, a thonging chisel (optional), 3/16-inch-wide calf lace, and a lacing needle.

Construction of the wallet is basically the same as for the checkbook cover at left, only the card holder is laced to one of the pockets first. After cutting out the four pieces of leather according to the dimensions in the drawing, punch an *even* number of holes around the sides and bottom of the card holder (⅛ inch from edges). Place the holder onto one of the pockets (grain sides up), mark and punch holes in pocket to correspond to those in holder, then lace the two together with the double running stitch. Now punch matching holes or slits around entire wallet body and three edges of each pocket (holes should be ⅛ inch from edges), then lace pockets onto wallet body. The whip stitch was used on this wallet, but you might prefer one of the other stitches described on pages 22-24.

WALLET BODY (CUT 2)
7½"
7"
POCKET (CUT 2)
1"
3¼"
CARD HOLDER (CUT 1)
3½"
3"

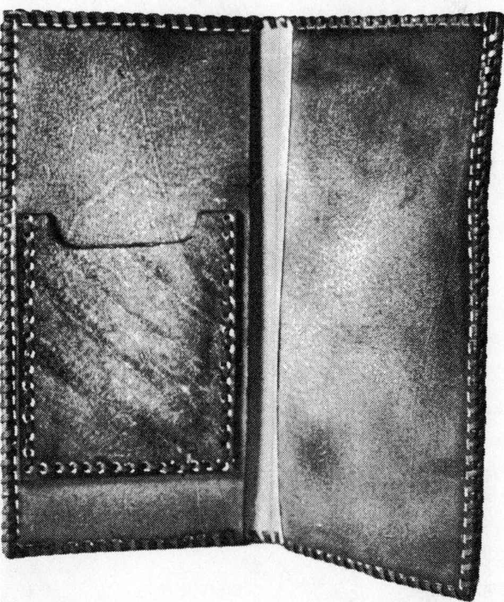

CONSTRUCTION of wallet is similar to checkbook cover, but lace the card holder to pocket before lacing pockets to body.

Women's Wallet

This women's wallet has a change purse plus four pockets—room enough to hold your money, credit cards, notes, and perhaps even your checkbook. The wallet measures 4 by 7 inches when closed. Four to five ounce cowhide was used to make this one, but you might want to try 2-3 ounce leather to make the wallet less bulky. Sheepskin, calfskin, or another type of leather would be a good substitute for the cowhide.

To make one like it, you'll need a utility knife or leather shears, a No. 5 round drive punch, snaps and a snap setter, a hammer, and a V-gouge (optional). This wallet was sewn together by hand with a double running stitch, using a harness needle and waxed nylon thread. A thonging chisel was used to make the sewing holes, but you might want to make them with an awl, in which case a stitch marker would be helpful to space them equally. If you don't want to sew the wallet, it can be laced. For lacing you'll need a thonging chisel or No. 0 or 1 round hole punch and ⅛-inch-wide calf lace along with a lacing needle. See pages 22-26 for more information on lacing and sewing.

Following the dimensions in the drawing below, cut out seven pieces of leather.

The unique pattern on the grain side of this wallet was achieved by batiking, but you might prefer to use another dyeing technique or apply stamped or tooled designs to the leather.

In assembling the wallet, sew the change purse to one of the narrow pockets after installing the snap in the change purse body and flap where indicated by circles in the drawing. (See page 27 for instructions on applying snaps to leather.) The snap post goes in the change purse body; the socket goes in the flap.

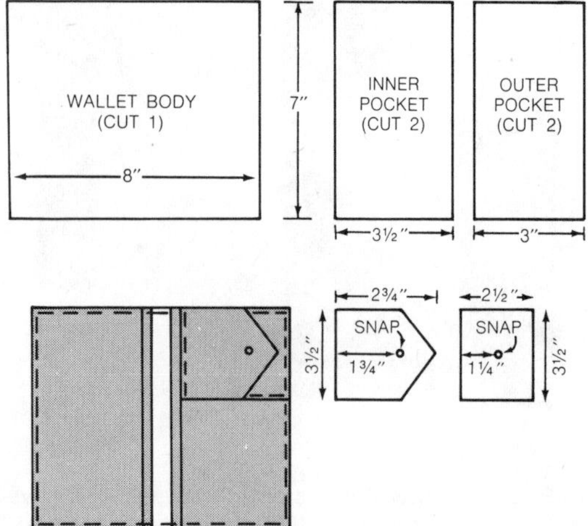

To sew the change purse body and flap in place on the pocket, position the parts as shown by darkened areas in drawing with the top sides (grain sides) of all pieces facing up.

After punching holes along the edges, sew only the inner edge of the change purse body and top edge of the flap to the pocket.

The four pockets of the wallet are sewn or laced to the back side (flesh side) of the body of the wallet at the same time, one above the other, grain sides up. At the same time also sew the two unsewn sides of the change purse body to the wallet pockets and body. Put the narrow pockets on top of the wider ones. Then, after punching corresponding lacing or sewing holes all the way around the wallet body and around three edges of the two pairs of pockets (holes should be ⅛ inch in from edges) lace or sew pockets onto wallet with the *back* (flesh) sides together. Any of the lacing or sewing stitches can be used (see pages 22-26).

Use a V-gouge to cut a groove down the inside center of the body if wallet does not fold easily.

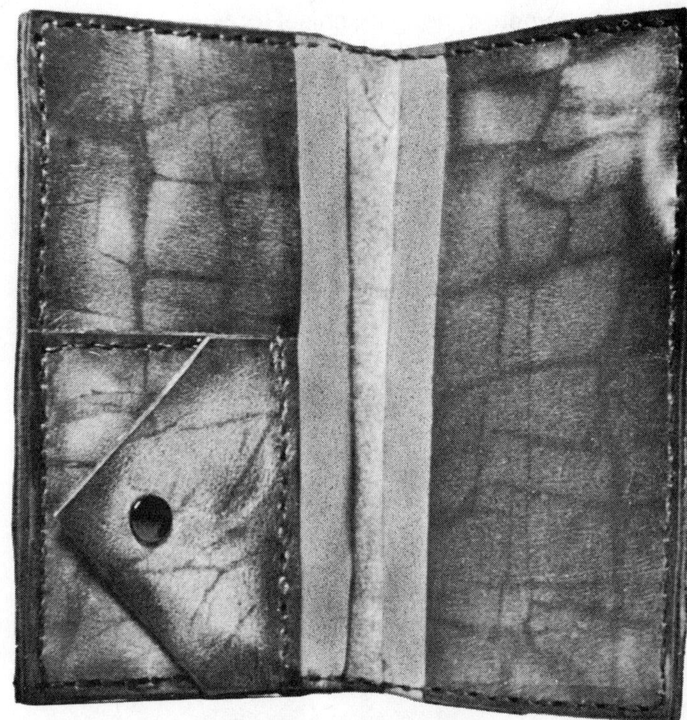

GAY STAFFORD

BEFORE SEWING the edges of pockets to body, sew inside edge of change purse and top edge of flap to an outer pocket.

STEVE SMITH

BILLFOLD CONSISTS OF four parts: two pockets and an inner and outer body. Pockets and body parts are laced together along side and bottom edges only. Pockets and inner body are also laced along top edge.

Men's Billfold

If taking out your wallet makes you wince, a handmade billfold like the one above might make the experience more often pleasureable. To make it you'll need 1-2 ounce cowhide, a thonging chisel, ⅛-inch-wide calf lace, a hammer, and a utility knife. A V-gouge is optional.

Cut the pieces of leather to the dimensions in drawing. If you want the window pocket such as this one has for a picture or your driver's license, cut it out of the center of one pocket (see darkened area in drawing). Decorate and/or dye the leather as described on pages 28-32.

To assemble the wallet, punch corresponding slits all the way around the two body parts and three edges of both pockets. Holes or slits should be ¼ inch from edges. Now place the two body parts on top of each other with bottom and side edges flush and the back (flesh) sides together. Set the two pockets, back sides down, on the inner body part. Beginning along the bottom edge of billfold, lace pockets and body parts together. Continue lacing across bottom edge, up the side, going all the way around the wallet. (Note that lacing along top edge of wallet back is only decorative: do not lace top edge of wallet back to the other parts.) The cordovan stitch was used on this wallet. Now lace the top edges of inner body and pockets together with the whip stitch.

CORDOVAN STITCH was used to lace the billfold together. Lace along top edge of outer body is decorative.

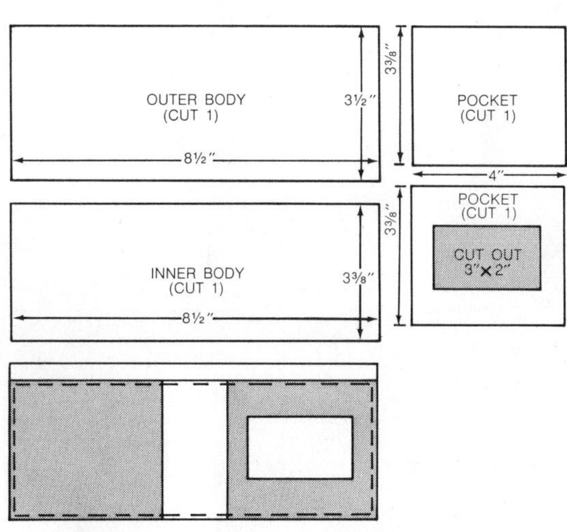

MARY LOUISE CARTER

THIS PURSE consists of four major parts: flap, front and back body pieces, and a gusset. Parts are laced together.

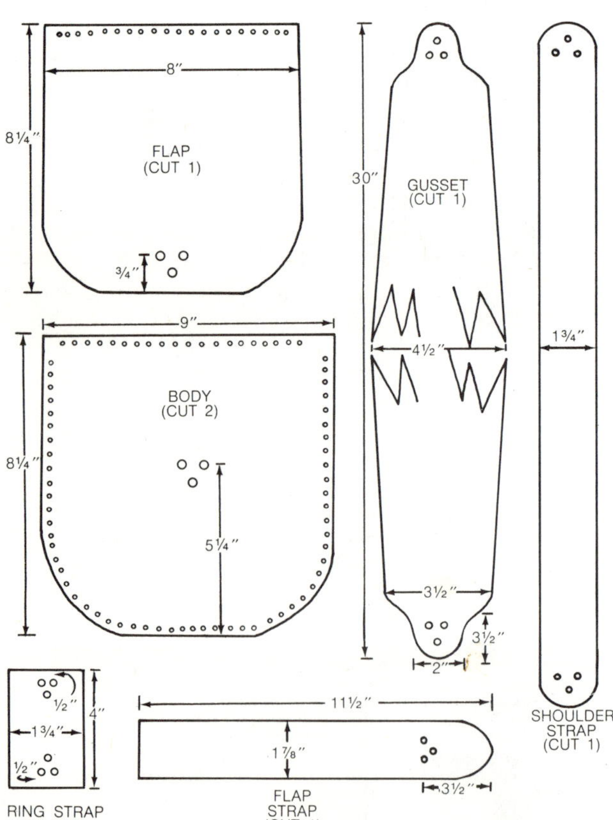

Laced Purse

The purse on the cover is not only handsome but easy to make, and its construction method is basic to all purses of this type; once you understand it, many modifications are possible.

Six to seven ounce oak- or latigo-tanned cowhide is usually used for purses of this type, since it has enough body to hold the shape of the purse but is not too heavy.

To make the purse, you'll need 2½ square feet of leather, along with 4 yards of 3/16-inch-wide thongs for lacing the parts together. Other tools and supplies you'll need are a 2-inch-diameter brass ring for the flap (available at leather shops), a utility knife or leather shears, a No. 5 round drive punch, a No. 3 edge beveler, and a round brass lacing needle.

Following the pattern diagram and measurements at left, trace the pieces for the purse onto the leather and cut them out. Parts include front and back of body (they are the same size and shape), the flap, gusset, shoulder strap (this one is 18 inches long, but you can alter it to suit your own tastes), the short band for the flap, and the strip of leather for the brass ring.

After you've cut out the pieces of leather, bevel all of their edges on both front and back sides.

Punching the lacing holes is next. Begin with those around the two body parts. Make 56 in both parts. They should be ¼ inch from the edges and ⅜ inch apart. (If you wish, punch the holes in one of the pieces and then use it as a pattern to mark holes for the other.)

Now punch holes in the gusset—56 along each edge. Again, they should be ¼ inch from the edges and ⅝ inch apart to match the holes in the body.

Next punch 20 holes along both the square edge of the flap and the top of one of the body parts. (This will be the back of the purse's body; the other one will be the front of the purse body.) Use the same spacing as in the body and gusset when punching holes in the flap. But since the body is wider than the flap, make holes in top edge of the *body* back ½ inch from the top edge instead of ¼ inch, and begin and end holes ¾ inch from the sides. Holes should be ⅜ inch apart.

Punch four holes in the square end of the flap band to correspond with lacing holes in the flap and purse back.

Other holes you'll need to punch include three in each end of the gusset and strap, three in the flap, three in the middle of the flap strap, and three in the front part of purse body and both ends of the strap that holds the ring. (Holes are indicated by circles in the pattern drawing.)

After all holes have been punched, decorate and/or dye the leather if you wish, as described on pages 28-32. The edges of this purse were dyed dark brown to give them a highlight.

Pieces of the purse go together as shown in the diagram below. Since all of the pieces are laced together, your work will go much faster if you use a lacing needle.

Begin by lacing the edges of the flap and purse back together with the running stitch. Be sure to put the flap on top of the body part with the smooth, outer (grain) side of each facing up. Knot one end of the lace and pull the other end up through the first holes in each piece. (The knot will then be on the underside of the leather and inside of the finished purse.) Continue lacing with the running stitch until you reach the seventh hole, place the flap band in the center of the flap, line up the lacing holes, and continue lacing the three pieces together. After you've gone through the last hole, the end of the lace should be on the underside of the body part; tie a knot in the end of the lace to hold it.

The end of the flap band is laced to the bottom of the flap as shown in the drawing below. Then fold the 4 by 1¾-inch strip around the brass ring and lace the ends (one on top of the other) to the purse front in the same manner as you did the flap band to the flap.

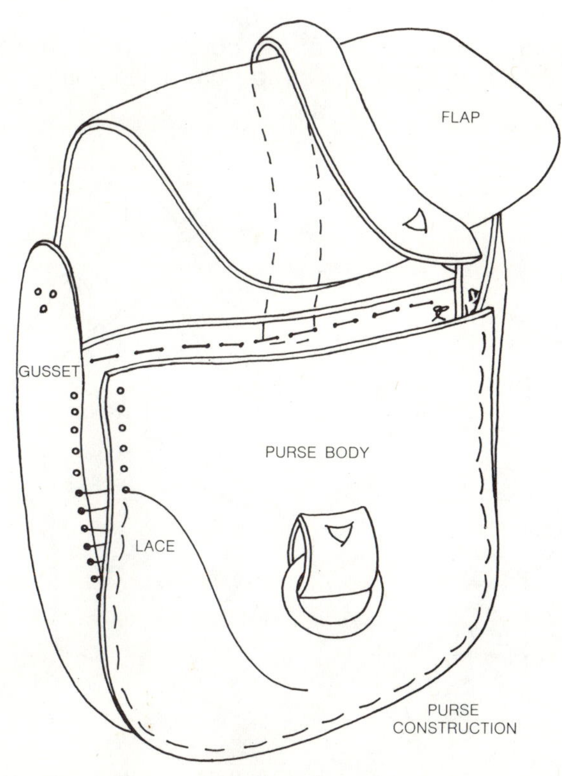

USE THE RUNNING STITCH to lace the flap to the top of the back body part and the front and back body parts to gusset.

You are now ready to lace the front and back body pieces onto the gusset. Lace the front body part onto the gusset first. Knot an end of the lace and, starting at one end of the gusset and top hole of body front, pull the lace through both holes, with the edge of the body on top of the gusset edge (front sides of each facing up) so that the knotted end is on the underside of the gusset and will be on the inside of the finished purse. Using the single running stitch, lace all the way around the purse body and gusset, bending the gusset around the body as you go. After going through the last holes, tie a knot in the end of the lace. (Like the first knot, this one should be on the inside of the purse.)

Lace the back part of the body to the other side of the gusset as you did the front. As you reach the end of the back piece, lacing may become difficult because of the limited working space inside the purse, but it won't be impossible.

Finally, lace the shoulder strap ends to the ends of the gusset as you did the ring strap and flap band.

Of the many possible modifications, the easiest are in the method of closure and flap shape. Variations of closure might include leaving the band off the flap and attaching the ring to the flap, allowing its weight to hold the flap down. Other possibilities are to use a harness button (page 27) instead of a brass ring, or you could lace a band of leather

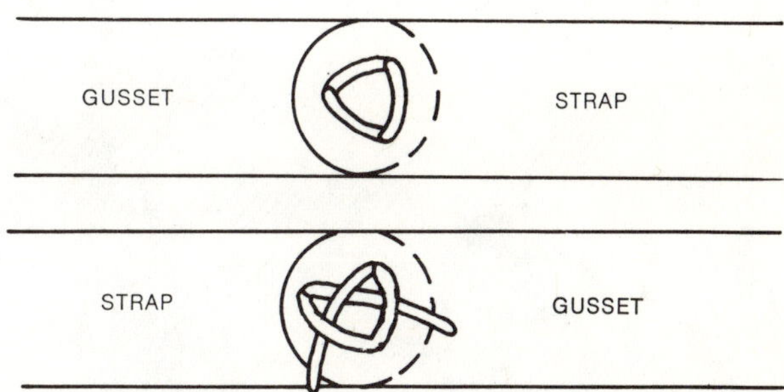

LACE STRAP ENDS to gusset as shown above. Lace should form a triangle on topside of leather. Lace ends are on bottom.

across the front of the purse at the same time you lace the body to the gusset and then tuck the flap through it. The flap can be cut to almost any shape you like.

If you want to alter the size or shape of the purse, keep two rules in mind. First, the body pieces must be the same size and shape and have the same number of holes. The gusset must be as long as the edges of the body around which it will be laced, and it must have the same number of holes along each edge as the body parts do. The second rule is always to cut an even number of holes in the parts. If you make an odd number, the end of the lace will be on the outside of the purse instead of inside when you finish lacing the body parts and gusset together.

PURSE PATTERN

7¾″ 11½″ 29″ 2″ 2″ ⅜″ 8″ 8½″ 2″ 8″ 8½″ 15½″

Box Purse

To make this box-shaped purse, you'll need a piece of 8 ounce latigo or chrome-tanned cowhide (or 6 ounce oak-tanned cowhide), a 4½-foot-long strap 1 inch wide, a utility or razor knife, a 1-inch slot punch or a No. 5 drive punch, a No. 3 edger, a V-gouge, and a hammer.

Following the pattern, left, cut out the piece of leather for the purse and then punch the 11 1-inch-long slots along each side and two in each of the tabs as indicated by ovals in the drawing. Bevel the edges of the leather, and, if you wish, decorate and/or dye the leather (see pages 28-32). The subtle sun pattern and cracks on this purse were done by a batiking process.

To assemble the purse, cut along each fold line (indicated by dotted lines in the drawing) on the flesh side of the leather with the V-gouge. Fold the purse along the four lines across the body to form the front and back of the purse. Then, after folding up the tabs at the bottom of the purse, fold the side flaps over one another to form the purse sides.

Now weave the ends of the strap through the slots, starting on the outside of the purse at the top slot on each side. (See drawing below.) Be sure to pull enough of the strap through the first slot to go all the way down the side of the purse, and leave about 3 inches extra at the bottom. Tension from the slots will keep the strap from pulling out.

GAY STAFFORD

ONE PIECE OF LEATHER and a strap makes this purse. The design on the purse was done by a batiking process.

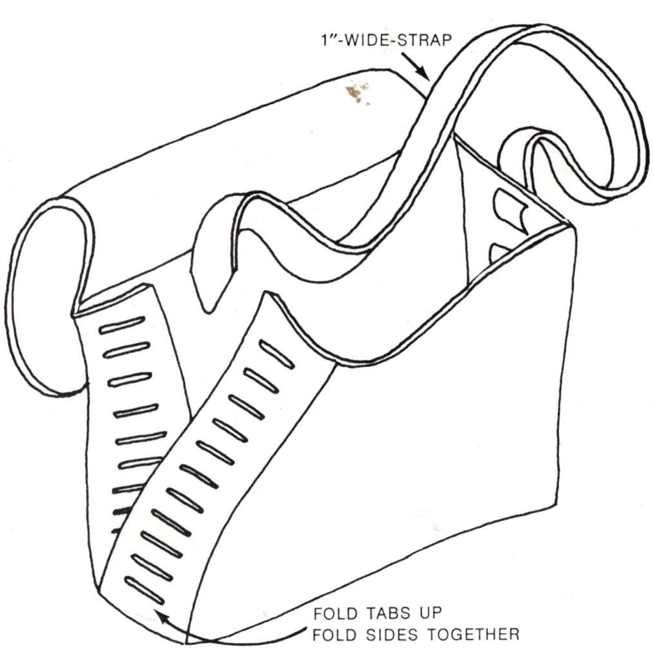

Round Purse

This firm purse was made from 7-8 ounce latigo-tanned cowhide, but if you prefer a softer one, make it out of 2-3 ounce sueded garment-type cowhide.

The pattern is simple, similar to that used with the laced purse on pages 48 and 49. Here, though, instead of lacing the parts together, you sew them.

The bead decoration on the flap of the purse was made by stringing beads on heavy thread, cementing the ends of the threads to the backside of the flap along the edges in the cut-out center hole, and then sewing a second piece of leather the same shape as the flap to the back of the flap.

To make a similar purse, you'll need a razor, utility knife, or pair of leather shears, a stitch marker, sewing needles or an automatic stitching awl, 3- or 5-cord waxed nylon thread, and cement.

First, cut out the pieces of leather: two pieces for the front and back of the body; a gusset; two pieces for the flap; and two pieces for the shoulder strap. If you want to add the strings of beads to the flap, cut out the oval in the two flaps, indicated by darkened areas in the drawing.

To construct the purse, first sew the front and back body parts to the edges of the gusset. (They go together in a similar manner as the body and gusset of the purse on pages 48 and 49, except that you sew, rather than lace, them.)

To sew the purse, you can use a blunt harness needle, the automatic stitching awl, or (if the leather is thin enough) a glover's needle. If you sew with a needle instead of the stitching awl, use the running stitch (page 25). Before starting to sew, mark the stitch lines (they should be ⅛ inch from the edges of the leather) with a stitch marker, so that stitches will be evenly spaced.

If you plan to add the bead decoration, string beads on a length of heavy thread or string that is long enough to go across the cut-out hole in the flap. Glue the ends of the strings to the backside of the flap with the beads in the open section. Then cement the inner flap to the surface of the outside flap and sew along outer edges and edges of the cut-out oval. Now sew the edge of the flap to the top edge of the back body part.

The strap consists of two strips of leather cemented and sewn together along the edges. After applying cement to the surfaces of the two strap sections, sew the edges. Then sew the ends of the strap to the top ends of the gusset.

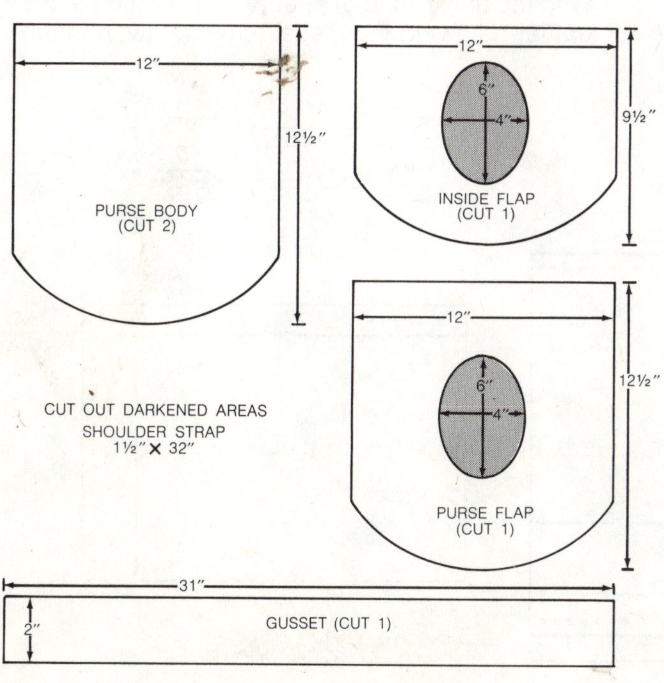

GAY STAFFORD

THIS PURSE is very similar in construction to the purse on pages 48 and 49. The bead decoration is optional.

SEVERAL DETAILS of this distinguished briefcase could be omitted for simplicity: the inside dividers, handle, harness button closure, and, if you just fold and lace the body against itself, the sides.

Sleek Briefcase

To make this distinguished briefcase, you'll need only four basic tools: a utility knife or leather shears, a No. 2 or 3 edge beveler, a No. 5 round drive punch, and a round brass lacing needle. Two harness buttons are used to fasten the flap closed; 2½ yards of 3/16-inch-wide thongs are necessary for lacing the case together.

The briefcase shown here was made from 4 ounce oak-tanned cowhide and has two dividers, made from 1 ounce oak-tanned calfskin, laced inside. If you'd like to simplify construction, the dividers can be eliminated; you could even leave out the two side parts, simply lacing the edges of the folded body together flat.

With the utility knife or shears, cut out the pieces of leather following the measurements given in the

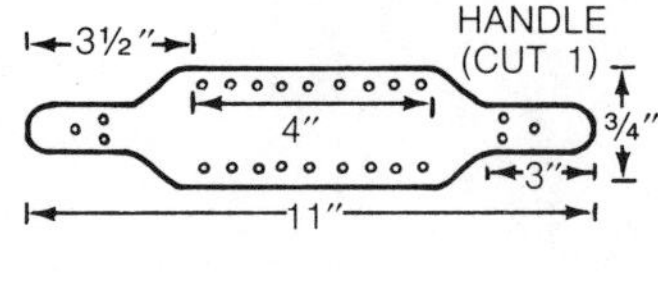

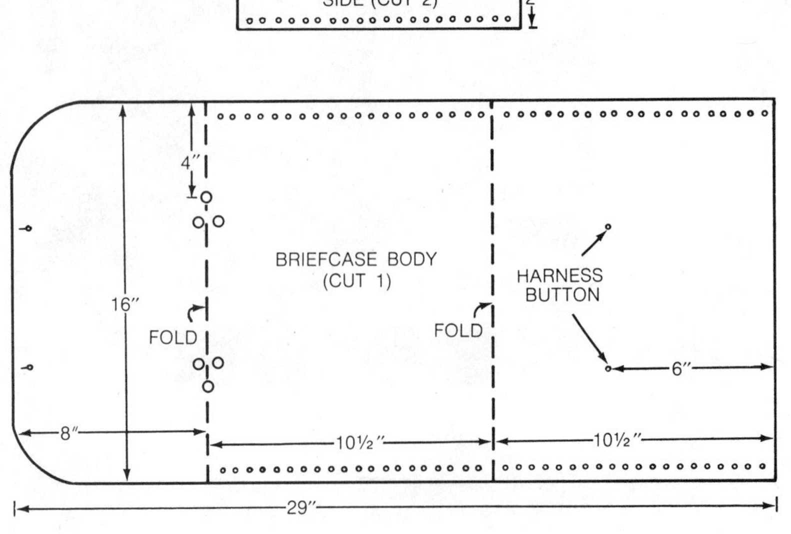

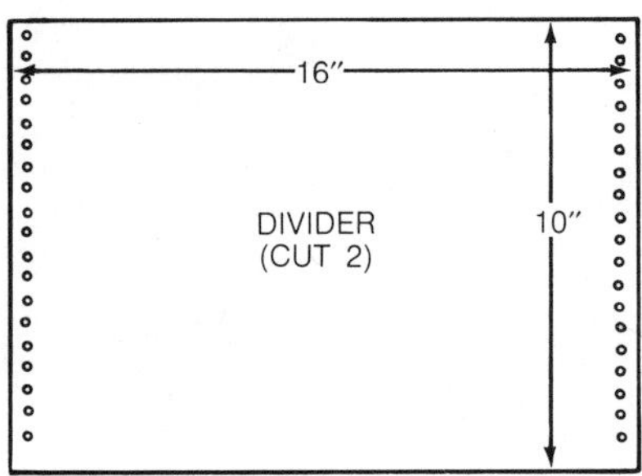

diagram. Bevel the edges of the leather. (The calfskin is too thin to require beveling.)

Starting at the square end of the body, measure and punch 20 lacing holes ½ inch apart along both sides; then skip one hole and continue measuring and cutting 20 more holes. Holes should be ¼ inch from the edges of the leather.

Now punch 20 holes, ½ inch apart and ¼ inch from edges, along both sides of the two side pieces. Cut ¼ inch off the bottom of each side piece so that the body of the case will fold neatly when parts are assembled. (Be sure to put this short end of the sides at the bottom of the case next to the fold in the body when you lace the parts together.) Also cut ¼ inch from the bottom of the dividers.

Punch the six holes in the body of the case (indicated by circles in drawing) for the handle and two more in the flap and body front for the harness buttons.

If you wish, decorate and dye the outside of the body, side pieces, and handle. Dye lace to match.

Before lacing the case together, screw the two harness buttons into the holes in the front of the case, as described on page 27.

The sides and body of the brief case go together as shown in the drawing below and are laced together with the single running stitch (page 23). Tie a knot in one end of a 1-yard length of lace, then pull the other end through the top hole of one of the side pieces so that the knot is on the smooth grain side of the leather. Then thread it through the top hole in the body so that the flesh sides (rough sides) of the pieces are against each other. Be sure that the short end of the side piece is at the bottom and will be next to the fold in the body.

Now place one of the dividers between the body and side, with the first hole of divider matching the second hole of body and side piece. (Again, be sure that the short end of divider is at the bottom of the case.) Continue lacing down the edge until you reach the last hole in the side piece.

Fold the body where indicated in the diagram page 52 by a dotted line and crease the edge piece inwards, lengthwise down the center. If you punched the correct number of holes (20) and started lacing so that the knot in the end of the lace is against the outside of the side piece, you should be able to just pull the end of the lace through the bottom holes to the other side of the body and continue lacing up the opposite edge. If you want to put in a second divider, insert it between the body and side as you did the first one before lacing through the bottom holes.

When you've finished lacing the entire side, the end of the lace should be opposite the first knot. Tie a knot in the end to secure the lace.

Lace the second side of the briefcase just as you did the first.

The handle of the case is made by folding the ¾-inch-wide strip down the center and lacing the edges together in the middle. As shown in the diagram, punch a row of nine holes, ½ inch apart and ¼ inch from the edges, down both sides of the handle. Holes should begin and end 3¼ inch from the ends of handle. Punch three more holes in each end. Dye the handle as you did the other parts, then fold the edges together and lace as shown in the drawing above. Attach the handle to the top of the briefcase with lace. (See page 49.)

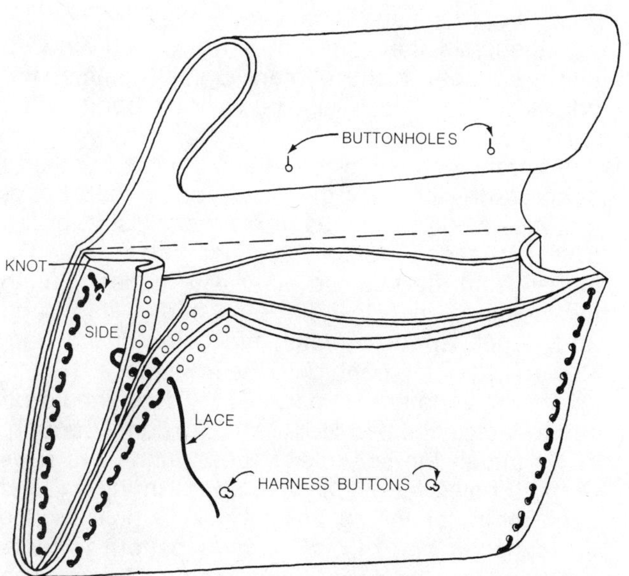

LACE BODY AND SIDES together with flesh sides of leather together. Knot in end of lace should be against side piece.

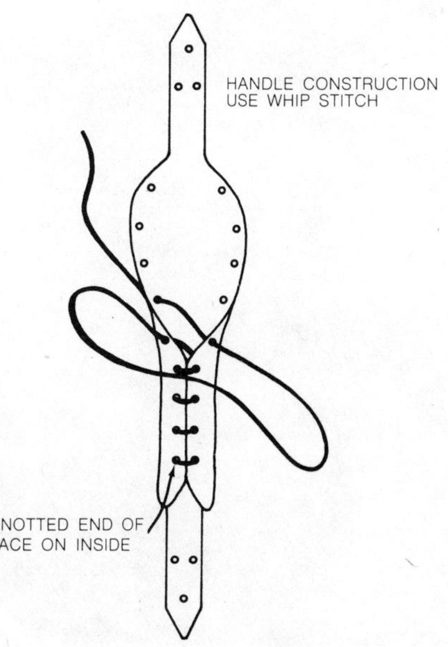

LACE EDGES of handle together with the whip stitch. Start from backside of leather so knot in lace won't show.

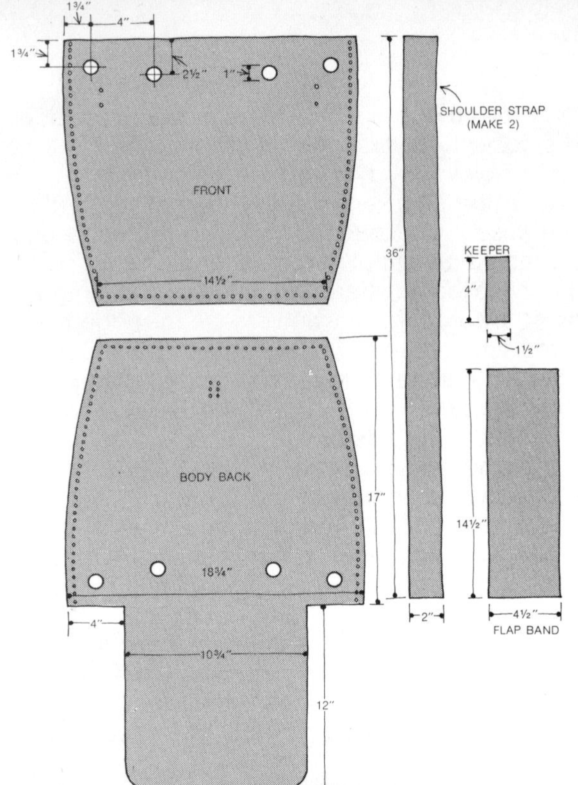

THE LEATHER WORKS

Backpack

For books, groceries, or a picnic lunch, this back pack is lightweight and soft—a stylish convenience for bicycle trips and hiking. If you're not traveling far, it slings over your shoulder and doubles as a shoulder bag.

To make one, you'll need a 4 by 2½ foot piece of top grain, 3-4 ounce, moccasin-weight garment-type cowhide. Take the pattern with you so you'll be sure of getting enough. About three yards of 3/16-inch-wide thongs are also needed. The only tools required are a pair of leather shears or heavy sewing scissors (garment leather is difficult to cut with a utility knife), about 12 rivets, a hammer, a No. 5 round drive punch, contact cement, and a metal surface for pounding the rivets on.

This particular backpack is made with the smooth, grain side of the leather on the outside, but if you wish, just reverse it to put the nappy, suede side out.

From the drawing, make a paper or muslin pattern of each part of the pack: two large pieces for the pack body; two 36-inch strips, 2 inches wide, for the straps; one piece 14½ by 4½ inches for the flap band; one piece 4 by 1½ inches for the keeper.

Place the pattern onto the leather, trace the outlines of each part and cut them out.

Before assembling the pack, fold and glue the shoulder straps, strap keeper, and flap band for extra strength and body. Draw a line down the center of each piece with a pen (on the suede side if you want the smooth side out). Brush contact cement onto the entire back-side of each piece, let dry, then fold the edges over from each side so that they meet in the center. Lightly hammer the edges as you fold to assure a good bond. (See photograph.)

After the cement is dry, attach the flap band and straps to the body of the bag. For the flap band, first measure 2½ inches in from each side of the front piece and punch two rivet holes: one 3½ inches from the top, the other 4½ inches. Punch two holes ⅝ inch in from each end of flap band and 1 inch apart to match the holes in the bag. Now rivet the flap band onto the front piece. (Riveting instructions are on page 21.) There should be some slack in the band for the flap to come through.

To attach the shoulder straps, punch two rows of three holes (about ½ inch apart) in the ends of each strap for lacing them to the bag, then use the punched end of a strap as a pattern to mark six points on the back piece, starting 3 inches in from the bottom edge (see drawing). Punch holes in the bag, then lace the straps one on top of the

FOR BICYCLE TRIPS or hiking, this knapsack is made out of 3 ounce cowhide suede and is laced together on the inside.

other to the bag with the lace going diagonally across the strap, then crossing over itself twice (as in photograph at center right). Tie a knot in the lace to hold it securely.

With the outer sides of the bag body together, pull the lace through holes punched in the edges of the bag, using the running stitch described on page 23 to lace the edges together. Tie knots in lace ends to hold them.

After lacing the bag, form the corners by pulling each one out into a V. Then, starting 2½ inches back from the corner, punch 4 holes through both layers of leather and rivet them together. (See photograph, top right.)

Turn the pack right side out. Punch one hole in each end of the keeper, then rivet ends together into a loop just large enough for the straps to fit through and slide it over the straps.

Bring one strap through the four holes on one side of the top of the bag, the other strap through the four holes on the other side. Lap the ends of the straps over each other at the front of the bag and lace them together. (Photograph, bottom right). Fill the bag and try it on for size: the straps can be adjusted to fit your shoulders by unlacing them, punching more holes, and relacing. Raw edges of the flap can be touched up with a felt marking pen.

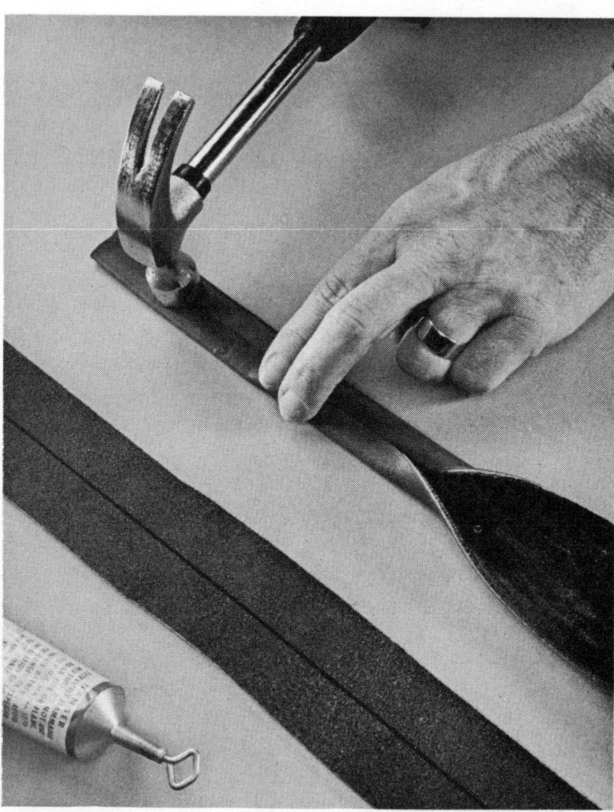

EDGES OF STRAPS are cemented in towards center of strap. To assure a good bond, tap leather lightly with a hammer.

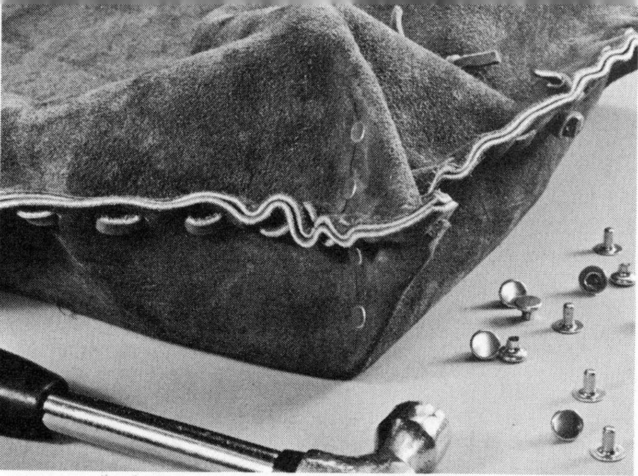

AFTER LACING right sides of body parts together, pull each bottom corner into a V and rivet as shown above.

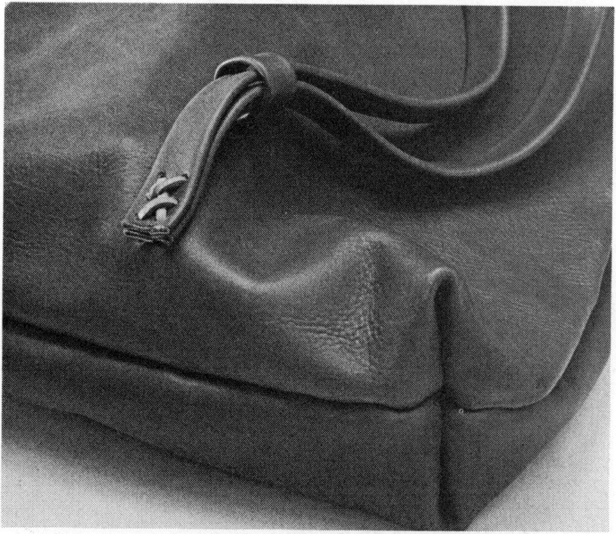

AFTER STRAP ENDS are laced to the bag, the right sides laced together, and the corners riveted, turn bag right side out.

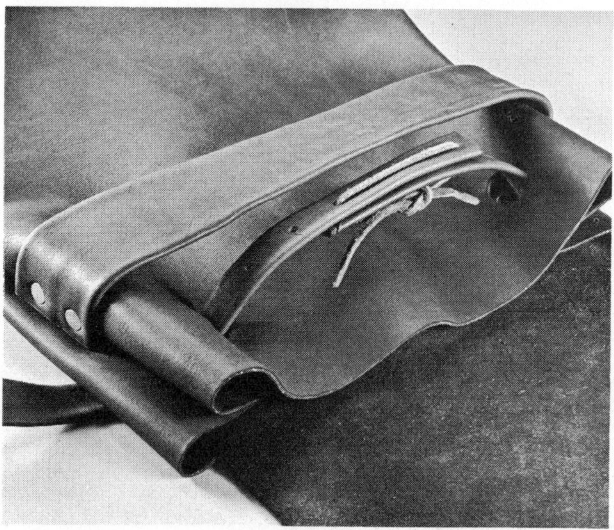

PULL THE ENDS of the straps through holes in the top of both body parts, then lace them together as shown above.

Travel Case

Though a large project, this suitcase is not nearly as difficult to make as it appears to be. It is all leather and has no cardboard or wood reinforcement: the thick, 8-9 ounce cowhide provides all the required strength and body. You should use latigo cowhide to make it. Since the suitcase has no locks, you may prefer to use it as a hand-carried travel bag. The one shown here is very roomy, measuring 21 inches long by 13½ inches high by 6 inches wide.

To make one like it, you'll need about 18 square feet of leather (a cowhide side should provide enough leather), two buckles, rivets, and 4½ yards of 3/16-inch-wide thongs. Tools include a utility or razor knife, a No. 5 hole punch (if you have a spring punch you'll also need a drive punch), a large brass lacing needle, a hammer, a metal pounding surface, a stitch marker, a harness needle and 5-cord waxed nylon thread, a No. 4 edge beveler, an awl or a No. 0 round hole punch, and a stitching groover (optional).

Cut out the pieces of leather as indicated in the diagram, right: the body, gusset, flap, handle, the four strips of leather for the straps, and two keepers.

Cut out the 13 by 8-inch opening in the body of the bag, indicated by darkened area in the drawing. The opening should be 3 inches up from the bottom edge of the bag and 4 inches in from each side. Next, cut the opening at the top of the flap for the handle to go through when the bag is closed. (Follow measurements in the pattern diagram when cutting openings.)

Bevel the edges, both top and bottom sides, of all the pieces of leather, including the inside edges of the interior openings.

All of the attachments (the four straps and handle) are riveted onto the bag. With the drive punch, first make 26 holes in the body and flap of the bag: five for each strap, and six at the top of the bag for the handle, indicated by dots in the pattern. Punch corresponding holes in the four straps and ends of the handles. Punch 11 lacing holes along both edges of the handle.

Next, punch the lacing holes in the body and gusset. With a pencil and ruler, draw a line around the entire body and gusset, ½ inch from the edges (see dotted line in pattern). Along these lines, measure and mark the lacing holes. They should be ½ inch apart and total the same in both the body and gusset. It is very important that you make an *even* number of holes and that there be the same number of holes in both the body and gusset; otherwise, the lacing will come out uneven, or the end of the lace will be on the outside of the bag when you finish lacing it.

After all of the holes have been punched, dye and/or decorate the parts as described on pages 28-32.

The parts of the bag are assembled as shown in the drawing, right. Before you begin lacing, however, rivet the straps (five rivets each) to the flap and body. Lace the edges of the handle together as described for the briefcase handle on page 53 and then rivet the ends of the handle to the middle of the suitcase body where you punched holes for them.

FLAP is sewn to the body about 1 inch up from the edge nearest the opening in the bag body.

WHEN THE SUITCASE is closed, the handle fits through a cutout slot in the flap. Secure flap with buckles.

RICHARD OSBORNE

The flap is sewn to the bottom edge of the body over the opening before the bag body and gusset are laced together. First, cut a groove in the flap down the stitching line with the stitching groover. (The stitching line is ½ inch up from the lower edge of the flap, beginning and ending about ½ inch in from the side edges.) Then mark the stitch line with the stitch marker. Position the flap in the center of the body over the body opening, with the bottom edge of the flap about 1 inch up from the bottom edge of the body. Rivet the flap to the body at the ends of the stitch line and then punch sewing holes for the blunt harness needle through both body and flap with the awl or No. 0 hole punch. Make holes in each of the marks left by the stitch marker. Sew the flap to the bag body with the double running stitch (page 25), using the harness needle and 5-cord waxed nylon thread.

With the flap sewn onto the body and the straps and handle riveted onto the flap and body, you're ready to lace the gusset and body together. Start by measuring 13½ inches in from each end of the body and drawing lines across the body (indicated by dotted lines in the drawing). Then measure 13½ inches from the ends of the gusset, drawing lines across it. These lines are the corner folds of the suitcase; you can use them to line the two parts up when you start lacing.

Since such a long distance must be laced, you can cut the lace into several pieces so that the entire length of lace doesn't have to be pulled through each hole.

Start lacing by lining up the lacing holes in the end of the gusset with the holes in the top of the bag. (The top of the bag is the space between the two dotted lines in the bag center.) Place the edge of the bag over the edge of the gusset. (Smooth grain sides of both parts should be facing up.) Then, after tying a knot in the end of the lace, thread the lace up from underneath the gusset through corresponding holes in gusset and body. Using the running stitch, continue lacing across the top edge of the suitcase.

When you reach the last hole in the edge of the gusset, fold the body and gusset as shown in the drawing below and continue lacing down the side. The corners of the bag may be somewhat difficult to fold square: bend the corners of the gusset under the body and pull the lace hard through the holes to bring the parts tightly together.

Continue lacing until you reach the end of the length of lace, then tie a knot in the end of the lace on the underside of the gusset (so that the knot will be on the inside of the completed bag). Begin lacing again through the next hole with a new piece of lace. Start as you did at first, on the underside of the gusset, so that the knot will be inside the completed bag.

When you've finished lacing all the way around the bag, knot the lace on the inside of the bag. Attach two buckles to the straps on the back of the bag, trimming the ends of the straps so that the buckles will be on top of the bag. Punch buckle tongue holes in the ends of the other two straps.

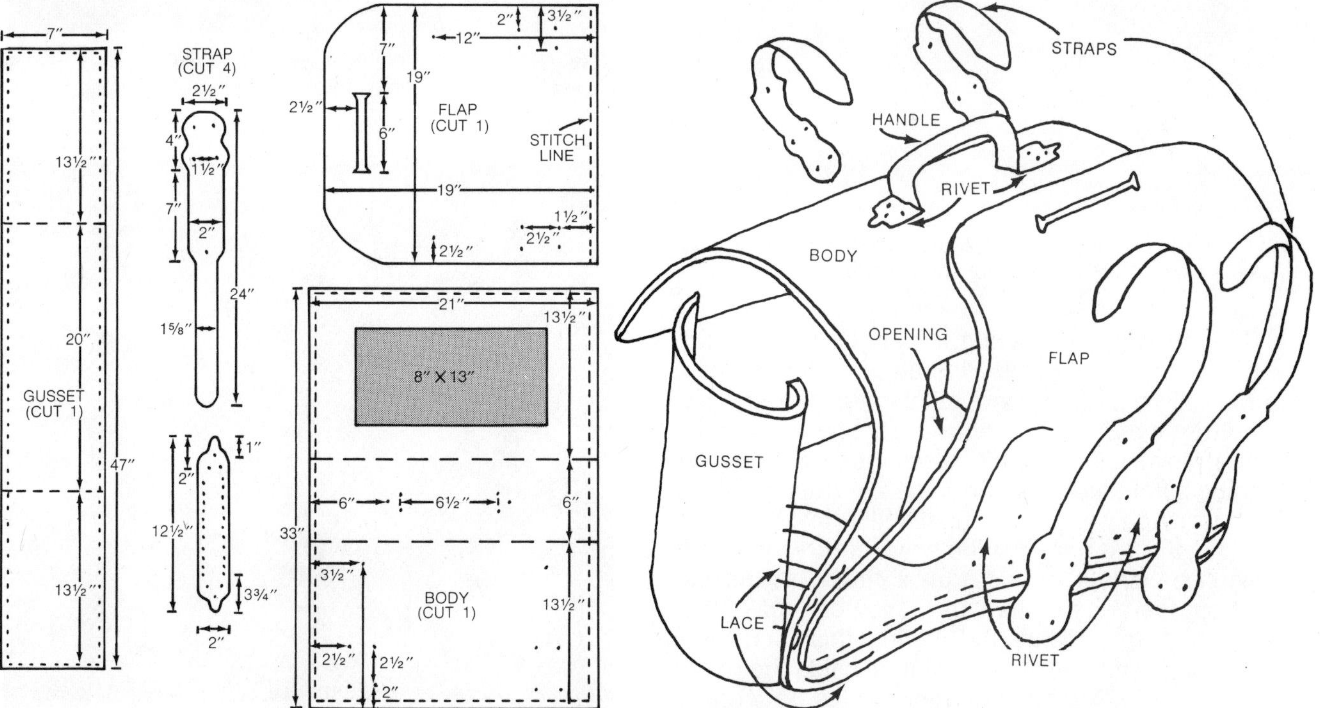

RIVET STRAPS to bag body and flap, rivet handle to top of bag body, then sew bottom edge of flap to edge of body below the opening. Use the single running stitch to lace the body to the gusset.

Cowhide Hat

Stylish on her, casual on him, this leather hat is made from a simple, two-piece pattern. To make one like it, you'll need a utility knife or leather shears, a No. 2 or 3 edge beveler, a stitching awl or sewing needle, waxed nylon thread, and a stitch marker. An 18 by 24-inch piece of 6-7 ounce latigo was used to make this hat (the head circumference was 24 inches), but 4-5 ounce oak-tanned cowhide could be used instead.

The hat consists of three pieces: the band, a brim, and the crown which is cut from the center of the brim.

Make the band first: it is a straight strip of leather 4 inches wide and as long as your head circumference, plus 1 inch for the seam. Cut the ends slanted as shown in the diagram, then bevel all edges and dye the band if desired.

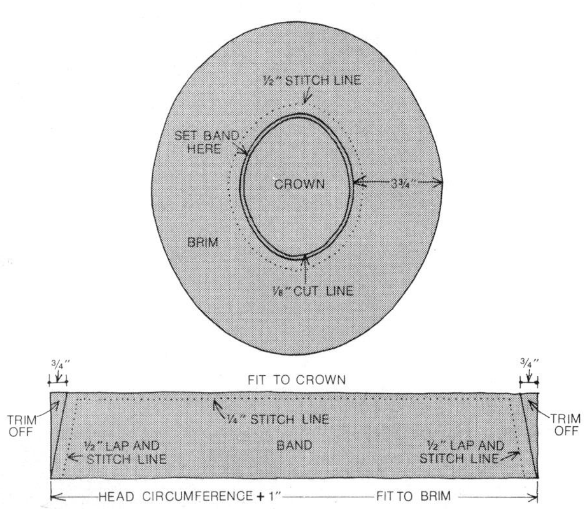

HAT consists of three pieces of leather: band, brim, and crown (which is cut out from the center of the brim).

Mark sewing lines along the edges of the band with the stitch marker as indicated by dotted lines in the diagram; then use a stitching awl or sewing needle to hand sew the ends together. If you sew with a glover's or harness needle, use the double running stitch described on page 23. (See page 25 for instructions on using the stitching awl.)

To make the brim, set the sewn band (wide end down) on the leather and draw a circle 3¾ inches out from the edge of the band. (You can make the brim larger or smaller by altering this measurement.) Draw another circle ⅛ inch inside the edge of the band. Cut around both circles to create the brim and the crown. Bevel the edges of the brim and crown and then dye the leather.

Set the crown inside the top of the band (the narrow end) and fold the edges of the band over to form a ½ inch overlap. After you secure the crown and band with six basting stitches, sew them together, removing the basting stitches as you go.

To attach the brim, first mark a stitch line ½ inch from the inside circle of the brim. Drop the brim over the outside of the band and sew the two together. The hat can be made rainworthy by treating it with leather waterproofing.

JILL ABELOE

SEW THE PARTS of the hat together with the automatic stitching awl or running stitch. (Note white thread in photograph.)

IF YOU TREAT the outside of the hat with a commercial leather waterproofing, it will be rainworthy as well as stylish.

Furry Cap

Sheepskin makes a fine, warm, woolly cap for chilly mornings, a day on the ski slopes, or winter camping. A cap like this one is easy to put together; the only tools you'll need are a pair of heavy scissors or leather shears, a stitching awl or glover's needle, and 3- or 5-cord waxed nylon thread.

For leather, you'll need sheepskin with the wool trimmed evenly to either ¼ inch long (as it was on the leather used for this cap) or ¾ inch long. You may have to buy a whole sheepskin (about 7-10 square feet) unless you shop at a store that will cut the skin for you. Be sure to make a pattern for the hat and take it along shopping so that you'll be guaranteed of getting enough leather.

The hat consists of two pieces of leather: a band and a crown. Make the band first. It is a strip of sheepskin about 9 inches wide and as long as your head circumference, plus about 4 inches. Measure and cut the band, then fit it around your head, lapping one end over the other. Pull the ends of the band as tight around your head as you want the cap to fit. Now, being careful to keep the ends in position, remove the band by pulling it over your head. Mark and then sew the band together, ½ inch in from the edge of the overlapped end. Sew the sheepskin either with the automatic stitching awl or with a glover's needle, using the single running stitch or the back stitch. After sewing the band, try it on and then, after making necessary adjustments, cut off the excess from the underlapped end.

To make the crown, first decide what shape you want the hat to have. The hat pictured here is oval, but you might prefer a round hat. Place the sewn band onto the smooth side of the sheepskin; form the band into the shape you want. (You must be careful that the band doesn't taper narrower at the top.) Trace around the band about ½ inch to the outside of it, then cut out the circle or oval of leather which will be the crown.

To sew the crown to the band, turn the band inside out so that the wool is on the outside. Place the crown over the band and fold the edges of the band and crown together so that the smooth sides of the leather are together. Sew the pieces together as you did the band, leaving a ½-inch seam allowance.

If the crown is oval-shaped, be sure to place it on the band so that one of the tapered ends is next to the seam in the band.

When the band and crown are sewn together, turn the cap right side out again and then turn up the edge of the band so that the wool will be on the outside of the cap.

BOTTOM EDGE of the cap can be turned up for a woolly trim, or you can leave it down to keep your ears warm.

JUDY WAITE

SHEEPSKIN CAP consists of a strip of leather with the ends sewn together and a round or oval piece sewn on the top.

Men's Sandals

Styles of sandals vary greatly both in construction method and strap placement. These men's sandals are very basic, and their construction can be adapted easily to other sandal styles, such as the women's sandals on pages 64 and 65 or a pair that you've designed yourself.

To make the sandals shown here, you'll need leather for the top and bottom soles and the straps. Generally, 6-8 ounce latigo or chrome-tanned cowhide is suitable for the top soles of men's sandals: 7 ounce latigo was used for the top soles of this pair.

The bottom soles of these sandals are made from 10 iron cowhide sole leather or "mechanical leather." (Irons are a special measurement designating the thickness of sole leather—10 iron leather is about 14 ounces.)

If you prefer, you can use hard-rubber sole material instead of leather for the bottom soles of the sandals. Hard-rubber soles offer much better traction than leather, but they must be cut with a jig or sabre saw.

The straps of the sandals are made from 6 ounce latigo. You'll need four 1-inch-wide straps (two for each sandal) to go across the top of each foot. You'll also need two ½-inch-wide straps for the heels of the sandals. Cut each heel strap long enough to go from the middle of one side of your foot and around the heel to the middle of the other side. Two short strips of leather—1¼ inches wide and long enough to go from the top of your foot to the beginning of your toes—are also necessary. All of the straps are cut to fit your feet when the sandals are fitted.

BASIC SANDALS have a strap going over the foot just behind the toes, another over the arch, and a third around the heel.

Besides the sole leather and straps, you'll need a razor or utility knife, a No. 2 or 3 edge beveler, a 1-inch-long slot punch or a No. 5 drive punch, a stitch marker (optional), contact cement, rivets, two ½-inch buckles, a hammer, 2 or 2½ ounce size shoe tacks (available at leather and shoe repair shops), and a flat metal pounding surface, such as a small anvil, block of scrap metal, or the side of a hammer head (not concrete, formica, or a brick). A wood file, rasp, or grinding wheel is needed for smoothing the edges of the finished sandals. Leather sealer and liquid conditioner are applied to the finished sandals to protect them from moisture and help break them in.

Sandal-making is not as difficult as it may seem. Basically all you do is cut the top-sole leather to the shapes of your feet, punch slots in the top soles for the strap ends to go through, and then, after fitting the straps through the slots in the soles so that they fit your feet and cutting the bottom soles, laminate the top and bottom soles together.

Cutting out the top soles. The first step in sandal-making is cutting the top soles of the sandals to the shape of your feet. Basically, this is just a matter of tracing around each foot either directly onto the leather or, if you prefer, first onto heavy paper that will serve as a pattern.

Standing on the smooth grain side of the top sole leather (or a piece of heavy paper if you want to make patterns), trace the outline of each foot. While tracing, stand with weight on the foot and hold the pencil straight up and down and right up against the edge of the foot. (If you make paper patterns, be sure to label them right and left foot.)

After tracing the outline of each foot, draw around each outline about ½ inch away from the foot outline. This ½-inch margin will give your foot extra room on the sole to adjust to the straps when you fit them. Excess sole is cut off after the sandals are fitted. Following the outer outline, cut out the top soles.

Positioning the straps. The next step is positioning the sandal straps over your feet and marking where they will go through the soles. Only the straps that go over the feet and through the soles are marked at this time. The heel straps are attached to the sandals after all other steps are completed.

Standing with one foot centered on the proper top sole within the foot outline, place the 1-inch-wide straps over the top of the foot. On this pair of sandals, one of the straps goes over the foot just behind the toes and another over the arch of the foot. The straps will probably fit best and be most comfortable if they cross your foot at a slight diagonal, following the natural contour of the foot.

Holding each strap in place on your foot, mark the top sole with a pencil where the strap ends will go through it. To do this, make a pencil mark on the sole on both sides of each strap and about 3/16 inch underneath your foot. (Hold the pencil at a 45° angle to mark under the foot.) Mark the positions of straps on both sandals before continuing.

Cutting slots for the straps. After the strap positions are marked on both soles, you are ready to cut slots in the soles for the strap ends to go through.

First, draw a pencil line connecting the marks on the soles, indicating the edges of the straps. Be sure that the lines are about 3/16 inch inside the outline of the foot. Using a 1-inch-long slot punch or a No. 5 drive punch, make 1-inch-long slots in the top soles along each of the lines.

Bevel the edges of the straps. If you wish, dye the straps and top surface of the top soles.

Fitting the straps. Once the slots are cut in the top soles, you're ready to fit the straps onto the sandal soles and adjust them to your feet.

The straps on this pair of sandals are woven through short, 1¼-inch-wide strips of leather that hold them apart and prevent them from slipping on your feet. Thread the straps through these strips before adjusting the straps to fit your feet. To do so, first put the ends of the straps through the slots in the soles, then place your foot into the sandal and pull the ends of the straps tight. Place a short 1¼-inch-wide strip over your foot on top of the straps and mark it where the 1-inch-wide straps cross beneath it.

Take your feet out of the sandals and remove the straps from the soles. Cut two parallel slits 1¼ inches long in the ends of both straps where you marked them. Pull the straps through the slits (see the photograph of the finished sandals on page 60) until the straps are centered on the strips.

Now you can fit the straps to your feet. Working with one sandal at a time, put the strap ends through the slots in one of the soles and then put your foot into the sandal. Pull the ends of the straps through the slots until the straps are fairly snug on your foot.

Lift your foot off the floor and wriggle it around a little bit in the sandal so that the sandal and foot adjust to one another and the foot finds the most comfortable position in the sandal. (If the strap ends pull out of the slots when you lift the foot off the floor, tape the ends under the sole with masking tape.)

With your foot back on the floor, retighten the straps as necessary so that they fit snugly. Since the straps will loosen up slightly as you break the sandals in, you don't want them to be too loose at this point or they won't fit later.

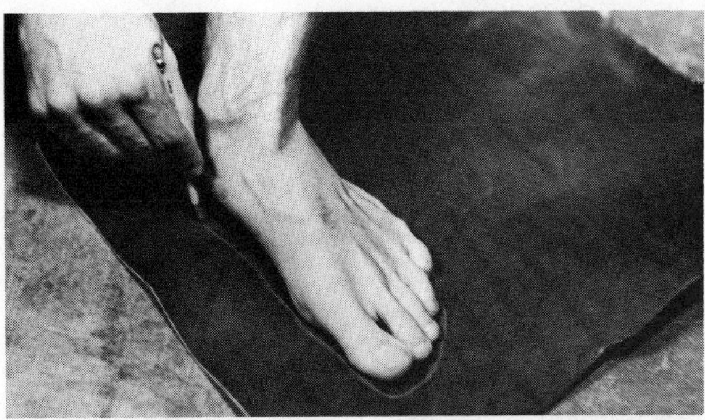

WHILE TRACING each foot outline, hold the pencil straight up and down and right up against the edge of the foot.

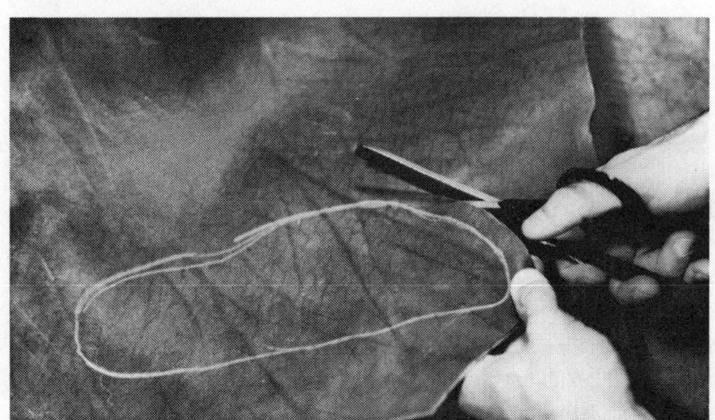

CUT THE TOP SOLES out with either leather shears or a utility or razor knife ½ inch away from the foot outline.

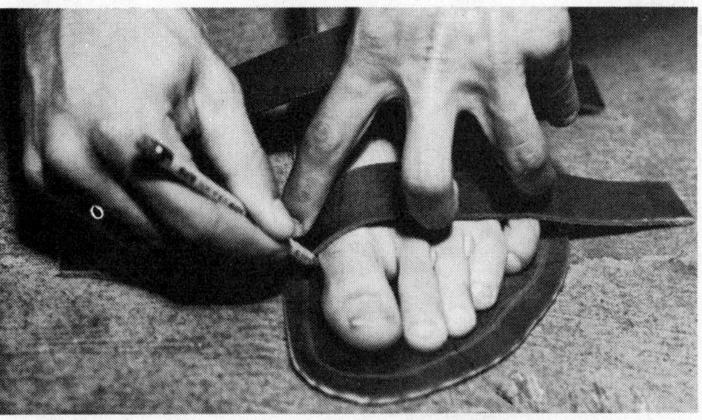

WITH STRAPS over your foot, make a pencil dot on each side of the straps to indicate where they will go through the sole.

When the straps are adjusted, mark each one with a pencil line where the ends go through the slots.

Before fitting the second sandal, continue as described below with the sandal you are working on. Then, after cutting the sole to fit your foot as described below, turn to the second sandal.

Final fitting and cutting the sole. After marking the straps, keep your foot flat on the floor and trace around it in pencil on the sole, holding the pencil straight up and down and right up against your foot as described above. This outline gives the exact position of your foot on the sole with the straps in place.

Now you can take your foot out of the sandal and cut the sole to the final size and shape. Cut around the foot outline, leaving about a ¼-inch margin outside the new foot outline. If your foot has shifted radically on the sole and there isn't room on it for a ¼-inch margin, you may be able to get by with as little as ⅛-inch margin. But before cutting the sole this close to the foot outline, try adjusting your foot and the straps to see if the foot will find a position more in the center of the sandal.

After fitting and marking the straps and cutting the sole of one sandal, turn to the other one and repeat the process.

Securing the straps. When the straps for both sandals have been marked and you've cut the soles to their final shape and size, cut the ends of the straps so that only about 1 inch of the ends are beneath the sole when the straps are in the correct position through the slots. Mark the ends of the straps in this way: right sandal, left front; left sandal, right front; (Rlf, Lrf) and so on to indicate which slot each end goes through. Remove the straps from the slots and skive them as described on page 18 so that they won't be bulky underneath the sole. (Start skiving about ¼ inch down from the marks on the sandals that indicate where they go through the soles.)

The straps on this pair of sandals were cemented to the underside of the top soles and then nailed to both top and bottom soles at the same time the edges of the sandal soles were cobbled together. On some sandals, however, the ends of the straps are sewn or riveted (instead of nailed) to the top sole to reinforce the cement bond.

Put the proper strap ends through the slots in the soles and pull them through the slots until the mark on each is just about to go through the slots. Apply contact cement to the underside of the strap ends and the bottom side of the top sole, pressing the strap ends inwards against the sole. Before continuing, allow the cement to dry for at least ½ hour. After cementing, if you wish to reinforce the strap ends, you can sew them to the top sole (pages 64 and 65) or punch a hole through the strap ends and top sole and rivet them together.

Cutting and laminating the soles. The top soles of the sandals are used as a pattern for tracing outlines for the bottom soles. Place each top sole against the underside (flesh side) of the sole leather (or the top side of the rubber soling material) and trace their outlines in pencil. Cut out the bottom

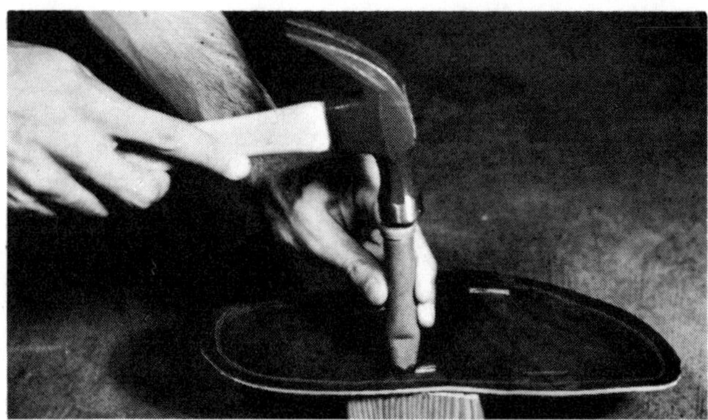

CONNECT THE DOTS on the sole marking the sides of the straps, then punch slots in the sole for straps to go through.

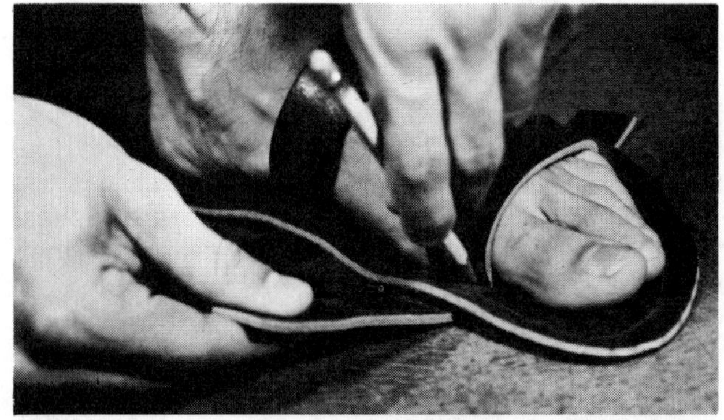

FIT THE STRAPS by pulling them tight across foot, through slots in the sole, then mark where the strap ends go through.

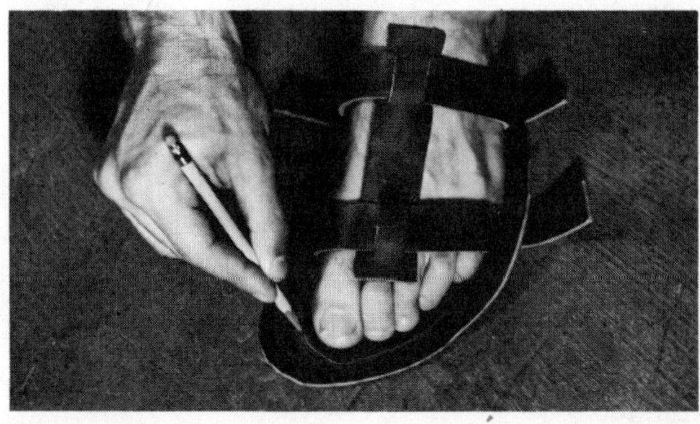

AFTER FITTING STRAPS, retrace foot outline. Trim off excess from the top sole ¼ inch away from foot.

soles: mechanical sole leather can be cut with a utility or razor knife; hard rubber soling material must be cut with a coping, jig, or sabre saw.

Apply contact cement to the entire bottom side of the top soles and the flesh (or bottom) side of the bottom soles, then press the two soles together.

Use the laminated soles as a pattern to trace heels for the sandals on the same material you used for the bottom soles. Cut out the heels as you did the bottom soles and then laminate them to the bottom soles.

Cobbling. Edges of the top and bottom soles of these sandals were nailed or "cobbled" together with small (2 or 2½ ounce) shoe tacks to reinforce the cement bond. Never use finishing nails or tacks designed for wood.

Apply the tacks about every ⅜ inch around the entire edge of the soles along the foot outline, traced on the top sole. (Mark the outline with a stitch marker to assist even spacing, putting a tack in every two or three marks.)

Pound the tacks all the way through both top and bottom soles against a flat metal surface (never brick, concrete, or formica). When the points of the nails go through the soles and strike the metal, they fishhook and curl back up into the bottom sole. Two or two and a half ounce size shoe tacks won't go all the way through the soles around the heels of the sandals, but they will provide enough strength to hold them fairly well. If you wish, use longer shoe tacks around the heels of the sandals only.

After cobbling the edges of the soles, put two tacks through the soles where each strap end was cemented beneath the top soles.

Fitting the heel strap. The heel straps on these sandals (some sandals don't have them) are applied to the sandals after the soles have been cobbled.

On the inside of each sandal, rivet one end of the ½-inch-wide straps on the outside of the straps that go over the arch of the foot. Rivet the strap ends about 1 inch up from the sole. Now put your feet into the sandals and bring the straps around your heel, cutting them off about ½ inch behind the arch strap on the outside of your foot. Apply a buckle to this end of each strap, as described on pages 36 and 37. Rivet the cut-off end of each strap to the arch straps on the outside of each sandal. After cutting the strap to size, punch holes in it so that the heel straps can be buckled.

Finishing. Sandals are finished by smoothing the edges of the soles with a large-toothed wood file, a rasp, or a grinding wheel. Wear gloves when finishing the edges because it hurts if you catch a finger tip on one of the tools.

Leather sealer is applied to the edges of the soles after they have been finished to prevent moisture from soaking between them.

If you apply a liquid leather conditioner over the entire sandals—soles and straps—they will break in faster and less painfully on your feet. Reapply the conditioner every month or so as necessary to prevent the leather from drying out and cracking.

AFTER BEING MARKED, strap ends are trimmed, skived, then replaced through slots and cemented to the top sole.

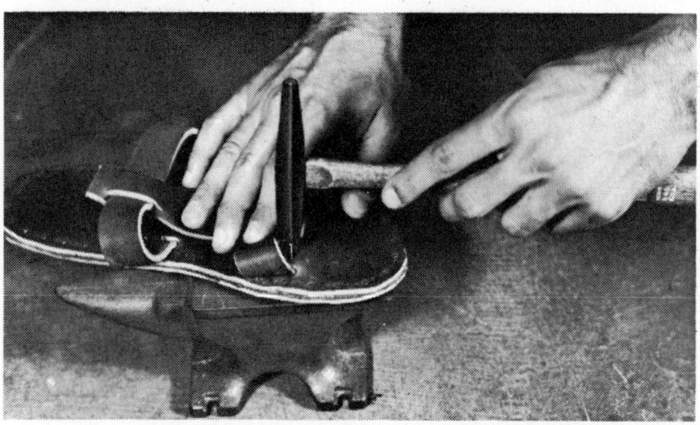

WHEN TACKING EDGES of top and bottom soles together, also apply two tacks where straps go through the top sole.

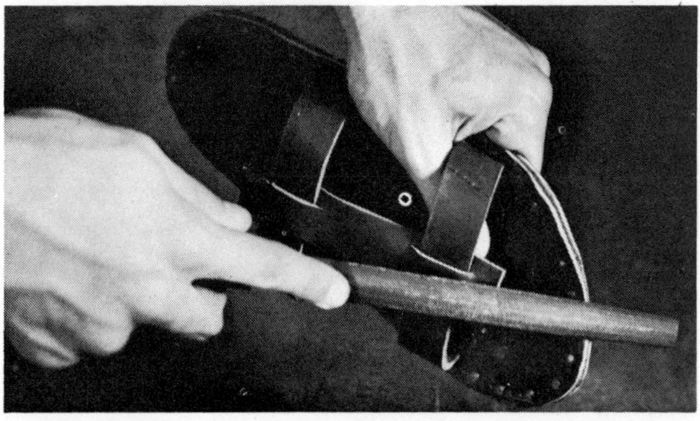

EDGES of the finished sandals should be filed smooth and even with a file, rasp, or on a grinding wheel.

Women's Sandals

The women's sandals shown on the cover of this book have an interesting strap design. Though they differ in several major ways from the men's sandals described on pages 60-63, construction of the two pairs is basically similar.

To make these sandals you'll need leather for the top and bottom soles. Get 6 ounce latigo or chrome-tanned cowhide for the top soles and 9 iron (10 ounce) cowhide sole leather—or hard rubber soling material—for the bottom soles. The straps are made out of 6 ounce latigo cowhide, but chrome-tanned cowhide could be used instead. Four straps are needed; they should be ¾-inch wide and long enough to go from your heel over the top of your foot to the tips of your toes, plus about 5 extra inches as a safety margin.

Tools include a razor or utility knife, a slot punch or No. 5 drive punch, a hammer, a No. 2 or 3 edge beveler, and contact cement. The soles of these sandals aren't cobbled like the men's sandals; they are only cemented. (You can, however, cobble them if you wish.)

The straps on this pair of sandals are sewn to the top soles instead of being nailed to the soles as the ends of the straps on the men's sandals are. (Note the dark thread line at the base of each strap on the top soles in the photograph of the finished sandals.) To sew the strap ends, you'll need an awl or No. 0 drive punch, 5-cord waxed nylon thread, and a harness needle.

When making the sandals, refer to the photographs and instructions on pages 60-63 for the men's sandals, making the necessary alterations described below.

Begin making the sandals by tracing the outlines of your feet onto the top sole leather and then cutting out the top soles, as described on page 60.

As shown in the photograph of the finished sandals (below left), the straps are split lengthwise almost to the end, making two sections to each strap. With the grain sides of the four straps facing up, use a razor or utility knife and straight edge to cut each strap lengthwise into two strips, one ½-inch wide and the other ¼-inch wide. As shown in the drawing below, two of the straps should be cut so that the ¼-inch-wide strips are on one side of the straps and the other two straps so that the ¼-inch-wide strips are on the other side of the straps. Do not split the straps all the way to the ends. Leave about 2 or 3 inches uncut at the end of each so that the straps can be adjusted beneath the sole. (If necessary, you can always cut the slit longer when you fit the sandals to your feet.)

With your foot on the sandal sole, inside the foot outline, place one of the straps over your arch with the uncut end on the inside of the sandal going under the arch of your foot. The ½-inch-wide section of the strap should be closest to your ankle and going over the top of your foot to the opposite side of the sole.

The other section of the strap (¼-inch-wide) goes across the foot just behind the little toe.

Holding the uncut end of the strap under the arch of your foot, make a pencil mark on either side of it on the sandal sole. Still holding the uncut end in position, mark the sides of the other two strap ends on the sandal sole. (One goes over the top of

MARY LOUISE CARTER

STRAPS on these sandals are partially split lengthwise into two strips that criss-cross over the top of the foot.

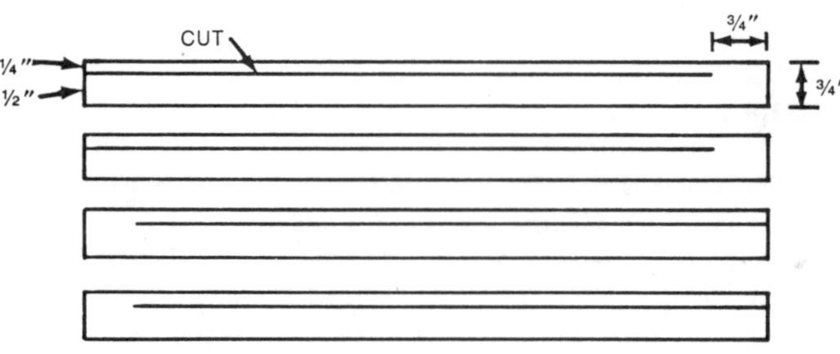

CUT STRAPS into strips—½ and ¼ inch wide—as shown.

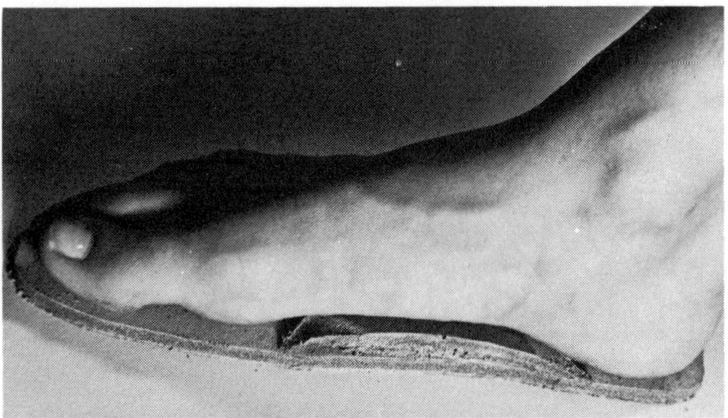

POSITION the arch comfortably while standing on the sole.

ARCHES can be carved from laminated pieces of sole leather.

your foot; the other goes across your foot just behind the little toe.) Remember: the straps should go through the sole 3/16 inch under your foot.

Remove the strap, keeping your foot in position on the sole. Place the other strap over your foot with the uncut end on the outside of the sandal ahead of the marks for the ½-inch-wide strip that goes over the top of the foot. Mark the position of the uncut end of the second strap onto the sole. Holding the uncut end of the strap in place, position the ½-inch-wide strip across your foot with the end going just in back of the big toe on the outside of your foot. Mark its position onto the sole. The ¼ inch strip goes in between the big toe and second toe. Mark its position on the sole. With the slot punch or a No. 5 round hole punch, cut slots for the sandal strap ends in the soles, just long enough for the strap ends to go through. Be sure to make the slots 3/16 inch inside the outline of your foot.

Bevel the edges of the straps and then, if you wish, dye the straps and the top soles.

Place the straps through the proper slots in the soles. As shown in the photograph of the finished sandals, the ¼-inch strip going over the foot to the little toe is woven between the other straps.

With your foot in the sandal, pull the proper ends of the straps through the slots until the beginning of the slit in each strap is just going over the top of your foot and the other ends cross over your foot comfortably. If necessary, you can cut the slit longer so that you have longer ends on the narrow sections to pull through the slots beneath the sole.

When the straps are pulled snug around your foot, mark each with a pencil line where it goes through the slot, as described on pages 60-63.

Adjust your foot in the sandals, as described on pages 60-63, and then retrace the outline of your foot on the top sole. Trim the sole, leaving about ¼-inch margin around the second foot outline.

Trim the ends of the straps so that only about an inch is below the sandal sole, then pull the straps out of the slots and skive the ends, as described on pages 60-63.

The ends of the straps of these sandals are first cemented and then sewn to the top sole. First, cement them down, as described on pages 60-63. (The ends of the straps going around the big toe should be folded towards the outside of the sandal.)

When the cement has dried, punch two small holes with an awl or No. 0 drive punch about ¼ inch apart through the ends of each strap and the top sole. Then make one running stitch through the holes—tying the ends of the thread under the soles.

Use the top soles as a pattern for marking and cutting the bottom soles.

Before laminating the top and bottom soles, cement arches to the bottom soles. (The sandals don't have heels, the arch lends a similar support.)

You can make arches yourself by laminating pieces of sole leather on top of each other and then paring the lamination to the shape of an arch as was done for these sandals; or you can buy pre-made arches at shoe repair and sandal shops. Pre-made arches come in various sizes, and you should take the sandals along so that you can choose ones that fit. Home-made arches can be pared down or built up with extra laminations until they fit.

To fit the arches, work with one sandal at a time. Position an arch onto one of the bottom soles of the sandals, then stand on the sole and move the arch around under the foot until it is in a comfortable position on the sole. (See photographs.)

When the sandal arch is comfortable, lift your foot up from the sole and trace its outline onto the sole. Take the arch off; apply contact cement to the arch's underside and inside the arch outline on the sole. Then press the arch onto the sole.

When the cement between the arch and bottom sole has dried for about an hour, apply cement to the entire surface of the bottom sole, to the top of the arch, and to the underside of the top sole, then press the top and bottom soles together.

The edges of the soles of these sandals are not cobbled together; just let the cement dry for several hours and then finish them. (page 63.)

If you wish, however, you can cobble the two soles together along the edges, following the outline of your foot.

Portfolio

PORTFOLIO folds into thirds when closed. Cut along fold lines with a V-gouge so that the body will fold flat.

STEVE SMITH

CORNER POCKETS of portfolio are laced to the edges of the body. The edges of center pocket are cemented to the body.

For prints, sketches, or notes, this portfolio is made from 8 ounce latigo cowhide, but chrome- or oak-tanned leather could be used instead. One piece of leather, 30 by 14 inches, for the body and another, 11 by 18 inches, for the pockets will be needed. Along with the leather, you'll need a razor or utility knife, a thonging chisel, a lacing needle, a No. 3 edge beveler, a V-gouge, and contact cement. You'll also need about 3½ yards of ⅛-inch-wide calf lacing. The stamping dies used to decorate this portfolio are optional.

To make the portfolio, cut out the four pieces of leather according to the dimensions in the diagram: one piece for the body, two corner pockets, and one center pocket.

Bevel the edges of the leather, then decorate and/or dye the leather. With the V-gouge, cut across the body piece (on the flesh side of the leather) where it will be folded (see dotted lines in the drawing). Now use the thonging chisel to make corresponding lacing holes along two edges of each corner pocket and two corner edges of the body. Then place the corner pockets on the flesh side of the body, grain sides up. (Note shaded areas in corners of body in the drawing.) Use the whip or cordovan stitch (pages 23 and 24) to lace the edges of the body and pockets together.

The center pocket is cemented to the middle section of the body with contact cement. Apply cement along the side and bottom edges of the pocket; press the pocket into place in the center of the body with the bottom edges flush. Lift the pocket up and apply cement along the cement line on the body, then press the pocket back into place.

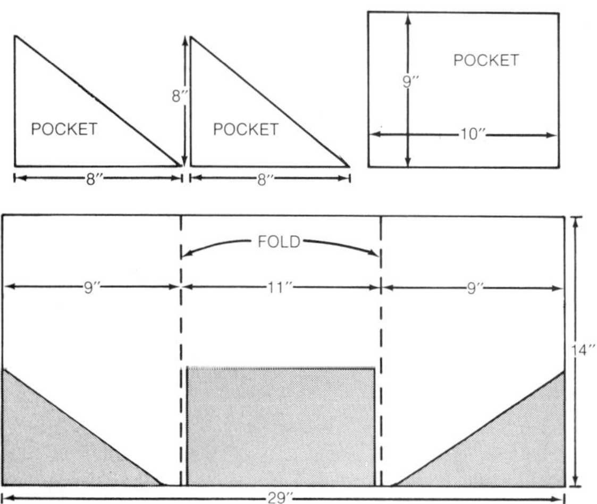

Chessboard

A laminated chessboard is not a particularly difficult project if you're a careful worker.

The board shown here consists of 64 individual squares of 8 ounce oak-tanned cowhide, hand dyed to two different colors, then laminated to a ¾-inch-thick plywood board. Each square is 2 by 2 inches square. Including its 2-inch-wide border, the entire board is 20 by 20 inches square.

To make one like it, you'll need a 20 by 20 inch piece of ¾-inch plywood for the base and 8-9 ounce cowhide. If you use latigo or oak-tanned leather, you can dye it to the colors you want at home (see pages 28-31); if you use tannery-dyed leather, be sure to get two contrasting colors, with enough of one color to make both 32 of the squares and the borders. Tools include a utility knife, a 90° triangle or T-square, a No. 3 or 4 edge beveler, and contact cement.

First, cut the four pieces of leather for borders 2 inches wide and 20 inches long. Cut the ends to a 45° angle so that they will form mitered corners. If you like, cut each border only 19 and 15/16 inches long to allow for a ⅛-inch-wide inlay at the corners. The inlay strips—3 inches long—are cut from scraps.

Cut the 64 2 by 2 inch squares out carefully, using the steel ruler and 90° triangle or T-square to assure straight sides and square corners. Do not try to use one square as a pattern for the others. From scraps cut four strips of leather—¾-inch wide and 20 inches long—to face the edges of the plywood base.

Bevel only the top edges of all the pieces of leather, except for the ends of the facing strips which also should be beveled on the backside at the ends so that they will form mitered corners. The narrow inlay strips are too thin to require beveling.

Dye the pieces of leather to the colors you want. Remember: half the squares should be of one color and the rest of another.

Start assembling the chessboard by cementing the four ¾-inch-wide strips of leather to the edges of the plywood board. Next, cement the 2-inch-wide border strips and inlays around the sides of the board.

Before cementing the squares to the board, it's wise to check their fit. Beginning at one corner, fill in one row of alternate colored squares at a time, eight to a row. If a square doesn't fit snugly against its neighbors without gaps, try another square in the same place before cutting a new one.

When you're satisfied with their fit, remove the squares and set them on a table in the same position they had on the board. Apply cement to the board for only one row of squares at a time. After applying cement to the back, fit each square into place again.

RICHARD OSBORNE

EACH of the 64 squares of this chessboard were individually cut, then hand dyed and cemented to the plywood base.

THE SIZE of the squares can be altered to accommodate your chessmen. Squares on this board measure 2 x 2 inches.

Hexagonal Box

The hexagonal shape of this box and its batiked pattern complement each other and create an interesting design effect. To make a box like it, you'll need two pieces of leather 10 by 10 inches, a razor or utility knife, an awl or No. 0 round hole punch, a harness needle and 3- or 5-cord waxed nylon thread, and a compass.

Start by making two hexagonal paper patterns—one for the top and one for the bottom of the box—as shown in the pattern drawing below.

First make the pattern for the top of the box. Draw an 8¾-inch-diameter circle and another circle with a 5¾ inch diameter inside it, using the same center point. Now measure the six sides of the box by drawing twelve lines inside the outer circle, alternating them 2¾ inches long and 1¾ inches long. Straight down from the center of each 1¾-inch-long line, make a dot on the inner circle. Draw lines from the ends of the 2¾-inch lines meeting at the dots as shown in the drawing. Cut out the resulting wedge-shape (the shaded areas in the drawing). Cut off the shaded area above each tab.

To make a pattern for the bottom of the box, draw a 9-inch-diameter circle and another one inside of it having a 5¾ inch diameter. As you did for the top of the box, draw lines around the inside of the outer circle, only make them alternately 2½ and 2¼ inches long. Mark the inner circle straight down from the center of each 2¼-inch-long line, then connect the ends of the 2½-inch lines to the dots. Cut out the resulting wedge-shapes, shown in the diagram as shaded areas.

You should now have the two hexagonal patterns for the box as shown in the drawings. Trace their outlines onto the leather and cut them out.

Punch matching holes along the edges of the six sides of each part. Holes should be about ¼ inch apart and ⅛ inch in from the edges of the sides. Bend the edges of the sides of the bottom part of the box together and, using the double whip stitch, sew them together. Sew the sides of the top of the box together in a similar manner.

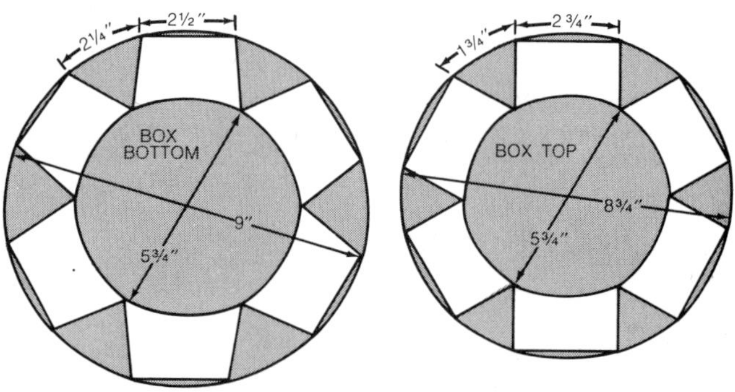

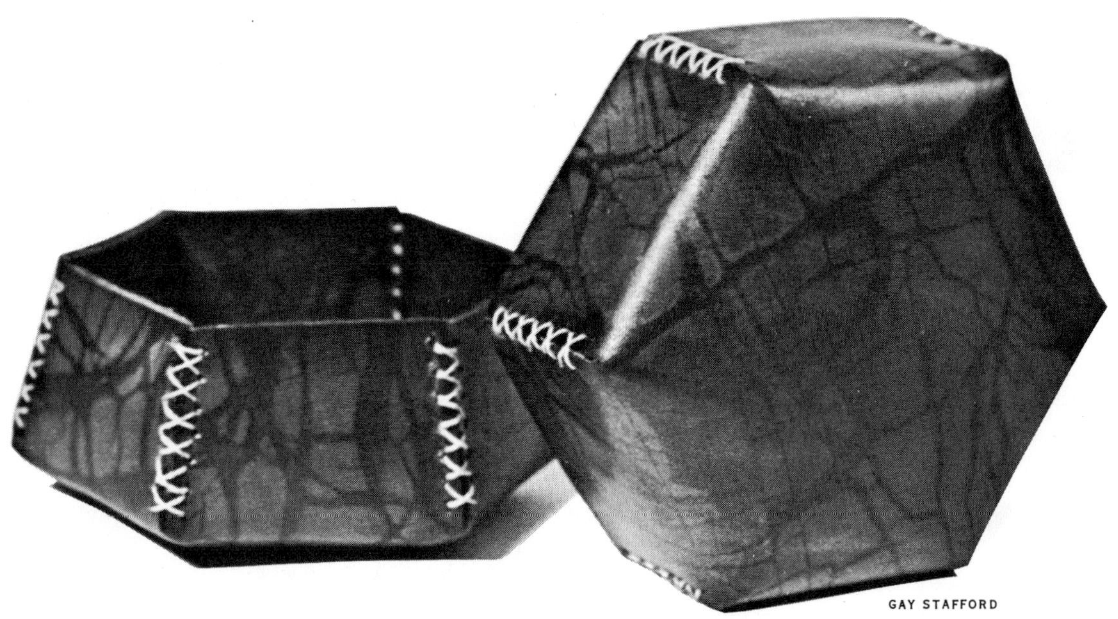

TO MAKE this hexagonal box, follow the pattern above and cut out two pieces of leather: one for the box top, another for the bottom. Punch sewing holes along the edges of the six sides of each and sew together.

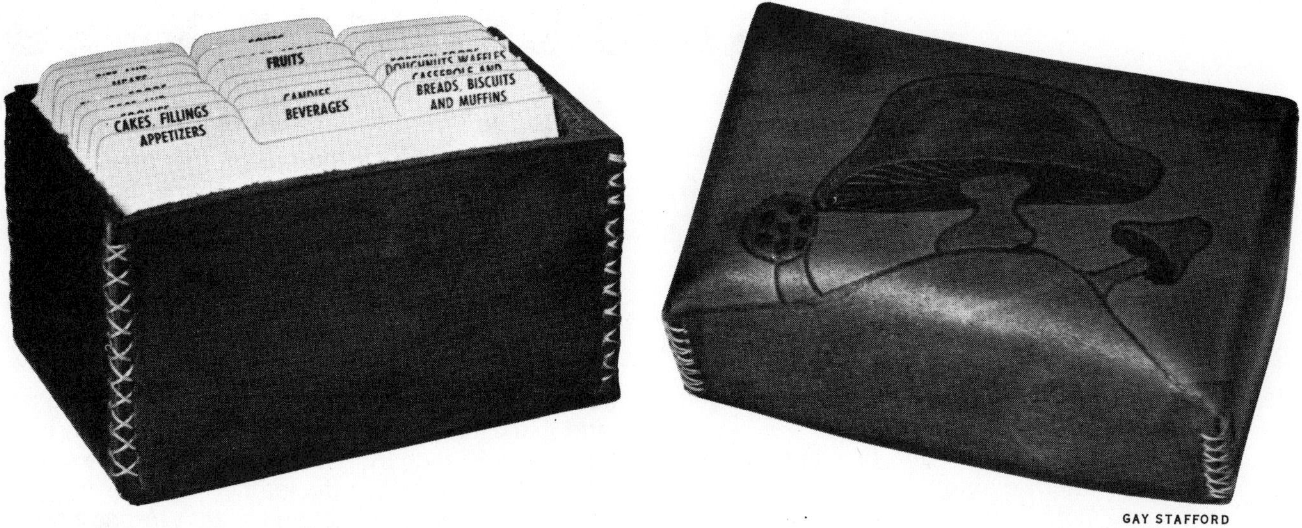

GAY STAFFORD

CONSTRUCTION of this rectangular box is similar to the hexagonal box. Follow the dimensions in the pattern below (or use your own) to make the box top and bottom. Fold the edges of the corners together and sew.

Rectangular Box

The leather box shown here measures 4 by 6 inches, is easy to make, and can serve as your recipe or cuff link box. Or it can hold spare change and odds and ends such as pencils, paper clips, and rubber bands. By altering the pattern measurements, you can make one like it in almost any size. Just remember that the top must be about ¼ to ⅛ inch wider and longer than the bottom so that it will fit comfortably over the bottom.

To make the box, you'll need 6-7 ounce latigo or chrome-tanned cowhide, a utility or razor knife, an awl or a No. 0 round hole punch, a harness needle and 3- or 5-cord waxed nylon thread, and a V-gouge.

Following the measurements in the pattern below (or using your own), cut out the two parts: one for the box bottom and another for the top. Now with the V-gouge, cut along the dotted lines shown in the drawing. The box sides are folded along these lines.

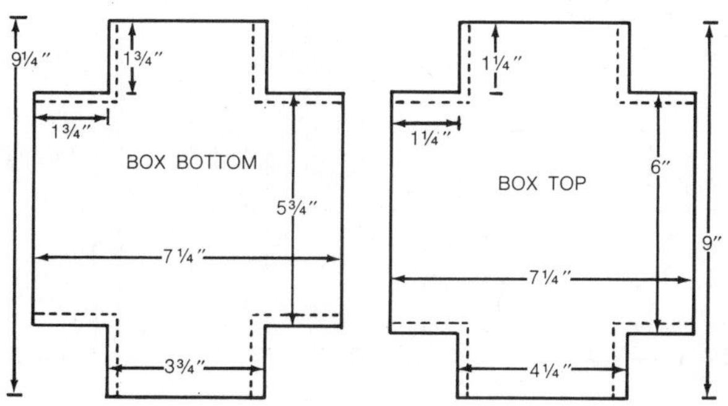

This box was dyed a light brown and then the mushroom was drawn on with colored felt-tip pens. If you want to do the same, just remember that felt-pen ink will fade if constantly exposed to sunlight. You can also use any of the other decorating and dyeing techniques described on pages 28-32.

After dyeing and/or decorating the box, punch matching sewing holes along the edges of the sides. They should be about ¼ inch apart and ⅛ inch in from the edges. Fold the sides of the box so that their edges meet, and then sew them together, using the double running stitch (page 24) and the blunt harness needle.

If you want to alter the size of the box, remember two points: 1) the length of the four tabs (or sides) determines how deep the box will be, and 2) the distances between the dotted lines separating the sides from the box bottom determine the length and width of the box. When making changes of your own, always make the *sides* of the top about ⅛ to ¼ inch shorter than those of the bottom; make the distance between the sides of the bottom (length and width) about ⅛ to ¼ inch shorter than those in the top, depending on the thickness of the leather you use.

Latigo Leather Vase

Though it won't hold water, this leather vase is still an attractive container for dried arrangements. This one measures about 9 inches high.

To make a similar vase, you'll need a razor or utility knife, a No. 5 round spring or drive punch, a No. 2 or 3 edge beveler, and a lacing needle (optional). For leather, get a piece of 4-6 ounce latigo or oak-tanned cowhide 14 by 24 inches. To lace the parts together, 3 yards of 5/32-inch-wide thongs were used.

Begin by cutting out the three pieces of leather shown in the pattern diagram: two pieces for the body and another for the gusset that goes around the body parts. To cut the body parts, first draw a grid on a heavy piece of paper, making the grid lines 1 inch apart. Then mark this grid wherever the lines in the drawing cross the pattern grid. Connect the points on the full-size grid and then cut out the pattern. Trace around the pattern on the leather. When you have cut out the parts, measure along the edges of the gusset and both body pieces and mark, then punch, lacing holes about ½ inch apart and ¼ inch from the edges. Bevel the edges of the leather and dye the leather if you wish.

To assemble the vase, tie a knot in one end of the length of lace and then thread the other end through one of the holes at the end of the gusset so that the knot is on the underside of the leather. Now, using the whip stitch, thread the lace through the top hole in one of the body parts. (While you are lacing, the backsides of the pieces of leather should be together.) After you've gone through the last hole, the lace should be on the inside of the vase. Tie a knot in the end of the lace to hold it. Lace the other body part to the gusset in a similar manner.

You can change the shape and size of the vase if you want. Just make sure that the front and back body parts are the same size and shape and that the gusset is long enough to go around the outside edges of the body parts. You also must be sure to make an equal number of corresponding lacing holes in the gusset and two body parts.

STEVE SMITH

LATIGO (oil-tanned cowhide) leather was used to make this vase, an attractive container for dried arrangements.

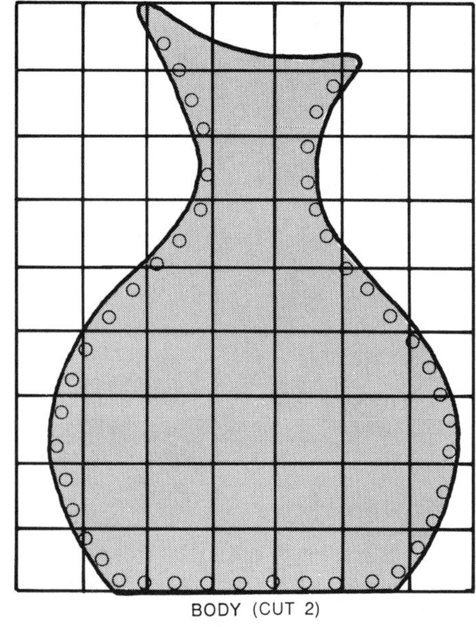

BODY (CUT 2)

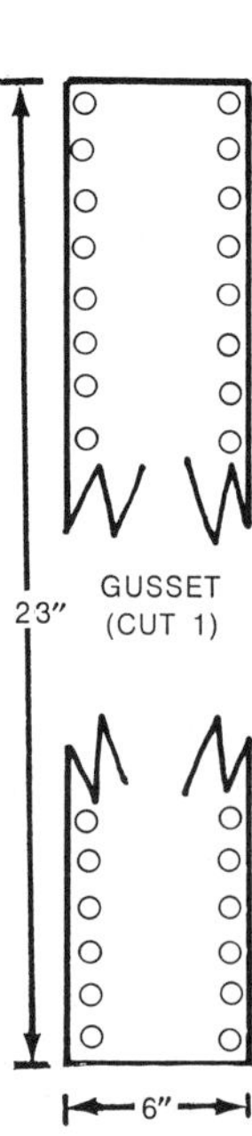

GUSSET (CUT 1)

Leather Fruitbowl

A centerpiece fruitbowl like this one is an interesting project. To make one you'll need a razor or utility knife, a compass, an awl or No. 1 hole punch, a harness needle, a stitch marker, and 3- or 5-cord waxed nylon thread. You should use fairly heavy leather—about 8-9 ounce cowhide.

Before starting to cut the leather, make a paper pattern for each of the parts. Begin with the top part of the bowl. As shown in the pattern at right, draw two circles, one with a 15-inch diameter, and another inside of it with a 10-inch diameter (use the same centerpoint for both circles). Now on the inside of the outer circle, draw six 6¼-inch-long lines, 1¼ inches away from each other.

Draw lines down from the ends of the 6¼-inch-long lines that meet at points on the inner circle midway between the 1¼-inch lines. Cut out the shaded, pie-shaped sections of the pattern.

To make the pattern for the bottom of the base of the bowl, draw a 7½-inch-diameter circle and then draw six 3¾-inch-long lines around it on the inside. Cut off the shaded parts of the circle above each line, creating a hexagonal shape.

On the leather, trace the outline of each pattern part and then cut them out: the bowl, the six sides of the base, and the bottom of the base.

To assemble the bowl, first mark the edges of the parts with a stitch marker. Mark only the side edges of the six flaps of the bowl, all of the edges of the six side pieces, and the six edges of the bottom piece. Do not mark the bottom of the bowl for sewing it to the base yet. Punch a sewing hole in each mark with the awl or a No. 0 round hole punch. Stitching lines should be ⅛ inch from the edges.

Sew the edges of the six sides of the bowl together, bending them upwards as you go, and using the harness needle and double whip stitch described on page 25. The edges of the leather should butt up against each other, not overlap.

Next, sew the six sides of the base together; you'll have to bend the sides inwards at the narrow point in each to get them to fit. Finally, sew the bottom section to the bottom edges of the side sections with the single running stitch.

Before sewing the bowl to the base, fill the bottom part of the base with coarse gravel or clay.

To attach the bowl to the base, set the bowl on top of the base and trace the outline of the base edges onto the underside of the bowl. Remove the bowl and mark a sewing line with the stitch marker on the bowl, ⅛ inch inside the outline. After punching a sewing hole in each mark, replace the bowl on the base and sew the two together.

GAY STAFFORD

FRUIT, NUTS, or a centerpiece arrangement might be held in this bowl—especially attractive on a patio table.

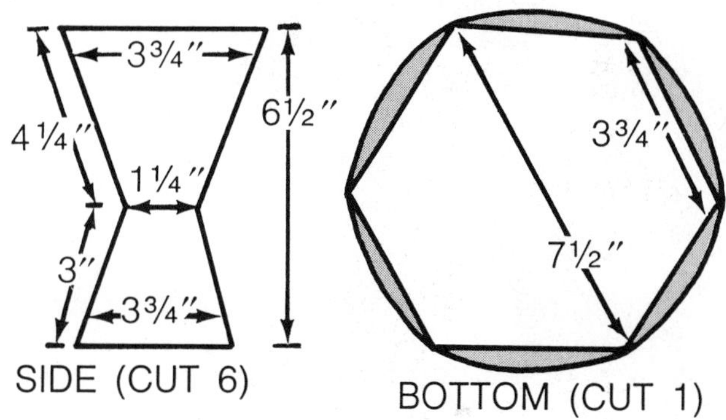

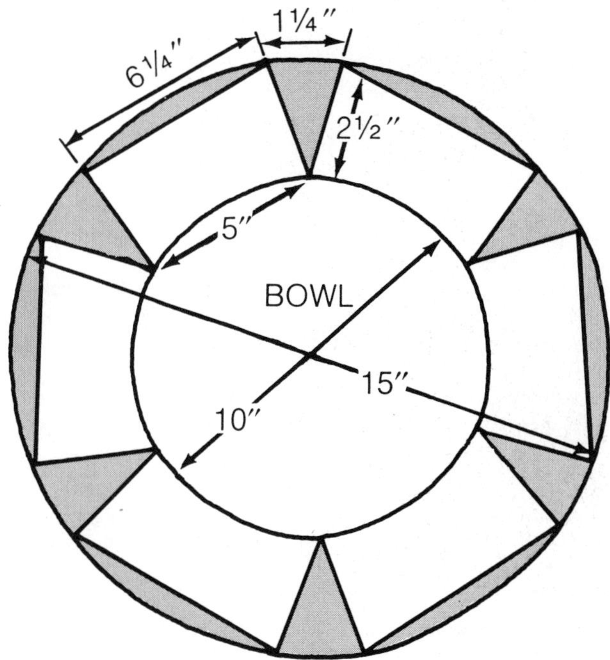

Bicycle Tool Bag

STEVE SMITH

HANDY FOR TOOLS, spare parts, and perhaps even a light snack, this tool bag laces onto the back of a bicycle seat.

A flat tire or loose gearshift cable might mean a long walk to a service station or garage unless you take tools along on your bicycle rides. Here is a small leather tool kit for wrenches, screwdrivers, and tube patches.

The bag ties to the back of the bicycle seat with thongs threaded through holes in the back of the bag. The flap is secured with two more thongs.

The bag is made out of 4 ounce latigo cowhide, but chrome-tanned cowhide would be a good substitute. You'll need a piece that measures about 7 by 22 inches. To lace the bag together, plan to use 1 yard of 5/32-inch-wide thongs.

A utility or razor knife, a No. 2 edge beveler, a No. 5 round hole punch (if you have a spring punch, you'll also need a drive punch), a hammer, and a lacing needle (optional), are the tools you'll need to make the bag.

Start by cutting out the three pieces of leather shown in the drawing: the bag's body and two gussets. Bevel the edges of the pieces of leather.

Punch the lacing holes about ¾ inch apart along the edges of the bag's body and the two gussets, as shown in the drawing. Now punch two holes in the back of the bag for lacing it to the back of the bicycle seat and two more holes, one in both the flap and the front of the bag, for tying it closed. If you wish, decorate and/or dye the leather.

The body and sides are laced together with the single running stitch, as shown in the drawing below. Start on the inside with one of the top holes in both body and gusset, lacing all the way around the edge. Repeat on the other side of the bag. Tie knots in the ends of the lace to secure them.

Now thread two knotted thongs through the holes in the back of the bag so that it can be tied to the bicycle seat. Knot one end of each of two more pieces of lace and thread them through the holes in the flap and front of the bag. Tie the ends together to secure the flap closed.

TOOL BAG CONSTRUCTION

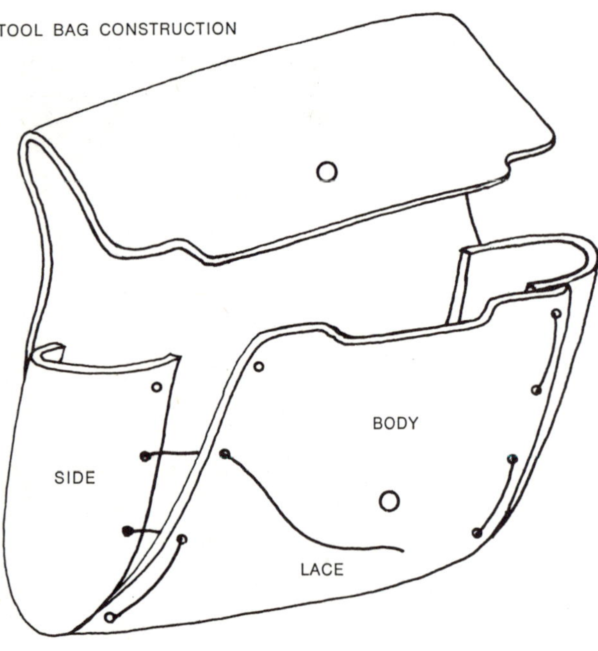

TOOL BAG PATTERN

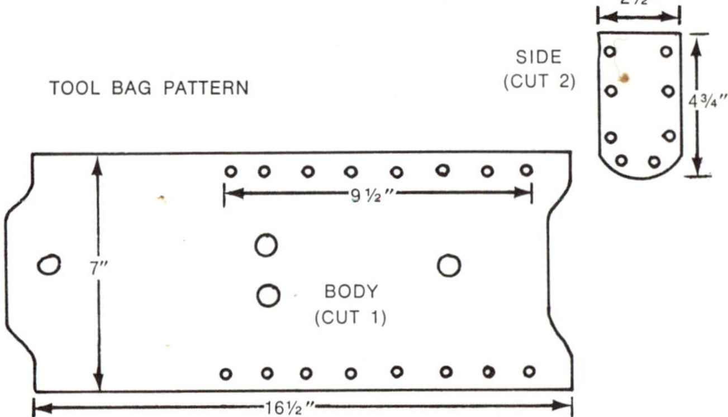

Sheepskin Apron

This leather workshop apron is sturdy, handsome, and easy to make. Though this one is made out of 3-4 ounce suede sheepskin, you could also use a similar weight of split cowhide. A 2 by 3-foot piece should be plenty, but take your pattern shopping with you to be on the safe side. You'll also need rivets, a hammer, strong scissors, contact cement, a No. 5 round hole punch, and a package of large eyelets and a setting tool.

Enlarge the pattern below to a size that fits you. Don't forget the pocket that is superimposed on the body in the diagram. (Heavy wrapping paper or muslin can be used to make a test apron.) Now place the pattern on the leather, trace its outline, and cut it out. From the leftover scraps, cut out three 3/8-inch-wide strips, 24 inches long, for drawstrings.

With the hole punch or scissors, make four holes at the top and sides of the body as shown in the diagram. Then attach an eyelet in each as described on page 28. Thread one end of a strap through each side eyelet, lap the ends over to form loops, then punch holes and rivet. Thread the third strap through both neck eyelets, adjust its length, loop the ends, and rivet as before.

To cement the pocket to the body, apply a line of cement around the back of the side and bottom edges of the pocket and, if desired, down the center to divide it in half. Set the pocket in place on the body, press lightly, then remove. Apply more cement along the resulting cement lines on the body. Let the cement dry for 10-15 minutes and firmly press the pocket back into place. Allow the cement to dry for at least 24 hours before using the apron.

JILL ABELOE

HOME CRAFTSMEN will appreciate this sturdy leather workshop apron. The generous pocket is cemented to the body.

Suede Pillow

ALYSON SMITH GONSALVES

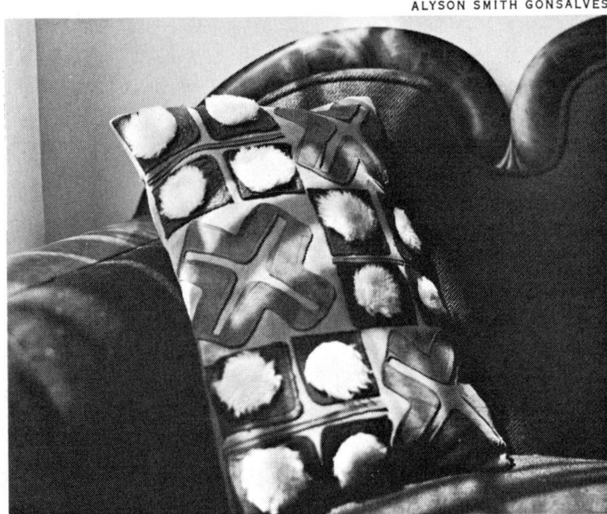

A SUEDE LEATHER PILLOW with an appliqued design on the front will lend accent to furniture, or decorate a day bed.

For a decorative accent to furniture, you might enjoy a leather pillow such as the one shown here. It is basically two pieces of 1-2 ounce split and sueded cowhide that is thin enough to be sewn on most home sewing machines (page 25) or with a glover's needle.

The decorative pattern on the pillow was created by appliqueing pieces of scrap leather (including sheepskin) onto the surface of one of the parts.

To put the pillow together, place the two parts on top of each other with the front sides together. Sew three of the edges together, either by hand or, if the leather is thin enough, on your sewing machine. Now turn the pillow right side out and fold the unsewn edges together, inside the pillow. Use the overstitch and sew halfway across the edge. After stuffing the pillow, finish seaming the edge.

Patchwork Necktie

BOBBI VANDERVORT

A LEATHER NECKTIE is both stylish and easy to make. This one has suede side of the leather out and a patchwork front.

Thin, 1-2 ounce, garment weight cowhide is suitable material for a stylish necktie. Necktie patterns are available in fashion magazines and fabric stores, or you can use a necktie that you already have.

Since a single layer of the leather is sturdy enough to hold the shape of the necktie, you don't need to double the leather over in back of the tie as you normally would with other fabrics. The leather won't fray, so no hemming of the edges is necessary. You just need to cut the leather to the shape of the tie.

The tie shown here was made with the suede side of the leather on the outside. Since suede tends to stick to itself as felt does, tying the knot is difficult. You might prefer to make a tie with the smooth grain side of the leather on the outside, lining the back to make tying the knot easier.

To make a similar tie, sew small squares of leather together for the front, attaching a triangular piece of leather to the end. Sew the other end of this patched section onto a longer strip of leather that composes the rest of the tie. An alternative to this patched-style is just to cut a single strip of leather to the shape of the tie without any piecing of small sections together.

Glasses Case

GAY STAFFORD

A GLASSES CASE is a folded piece of sueded cowhide with the bottom and side edges sewn together; decoration optional.

This glasses case is just a 6½ by 6½-inch piece of 1-2 ounce sueded cowhide, folded in the center and sewn along the bottom and side edges. The corners were cut to a rounded shape and the top edge was cut to a slant after the case was sewn.

To decorate the case like the one shown, just cut out a shape from the front half of the leather before folding and sewing the edges. On the inside of the leather, sew a piece of different colored suede over the cut-out area. If you wish, continue the process and cut out the sewn inlay, then sew another piece of suede behind it. After appliqueing, fold the leather along the center and sew the bottom and side edges together. Sew the leather on your sewing machine or with a glover's needle.

The opening at the top of this case was reinforced by sewing a piece of suede, 6½ inches long by 2 inches wide, to the inside along the top edge before the case was sewn.

Teddy the Bear

ALYSON SMITH GONSALVES

THIS BEAR is made out of cowhide suede. He sports a black leather nose, colored suede eyes, and a smile.

A stuffed bear, or any other stuffed animal, is a playful leather project. If you use thin, 1-2 ounce sueded cowhide, you can make the stuffed animal out of leather just as you would make him out of any other fabric.

Patterns for stuffed animals and dolls can be found in sewing magazines, fabric stores, doll and toy making books, and craft articles in your local newspaper supplement or family magazine.

After selecting a pattern you like, follow it to cut out the necessary pieces of leather. Then follow the pattern instructions to assemble the parts of the animal. You may be able to sew the leather on your home sewing machine as described on page 25. If not, use a glover's needle (page 16) and sew the parts together by hand using the backstitch or overstitch.

Some special features that you might want to include on the stuffed animal to personalize it are a black leather nose, a red leather tongue, and blue leather eyes.

Since leather is thicker and has more body than most other fabrics, you may be able to save time and effort by making the ears and tail out of single pieces of leather rather than out of two pieces that have been sewn together and stuffed.

Hanging Containers

Hanging containers made out of leather, such as the basket on page 35, are highly versatile. Below are two different ideas that you might like to try: a hanging spice rack and a wall secretary.

The spice rack (below left) is made entirely out of scraps. The ragged right edge is the natural edge of the hide; the other edge was cut to form a rugged symmetry. To make one like it, you'll need only some scraps of leather, a cutting tool, a hole punch, and thongs.

This one is made to hold three spice jars, but if longer pieces of leather were used, it could hold more.

First, position the spice jars in a row on a piece of thick (8 ounce) leather. Cut the edges of the leather around the jars into a shape you like. With the jars still in position, place a long strip of flexible leather (1-2 ounce suede) over them.

Between each jar, press the strip against the backing piece of leather, punch two holes in both the suede and backing, then lace them together to create a pocket for each jar. (Knot the ends of the pieces of lace to hold them.)

Each jar rests on a piece of lace knotted through a hole punched at the bottom edge of each pocket and another punched in the backing leather.

A wall secretary (such as the one shown below right) could hold note pads and pencils and be hung on the wall near a phone. You could place it near a desk and file envelopes, stationery, and letters in the pockets. Or you could make many different-shaped pockets to store anything from scissors to a bunch of attractive dried leaves.

You can make the secretary any size or shape you like and have wall space for. Basically it is just a single piece of heavy (8 ounce) leather for the backing with smaller pieces of leather laced or riveted onto it to form pockets.

The pockets can be made in several ways and styles. For large pockets for papers, envelopes, and letters, just lace or rivet two or three edges of a piece of leather onto the backing. Lacing or riveting the ends of narrow strips to the backing forms loops for pencils, pens, scissors, and other utensils. If you want pockets with sides, use the whip stitch to lace the edges of two pieces of leather together, then pull them apart to form a 45° angle and lace the edge of the side piece to the backing.

WILLIAM J. SHELLEY

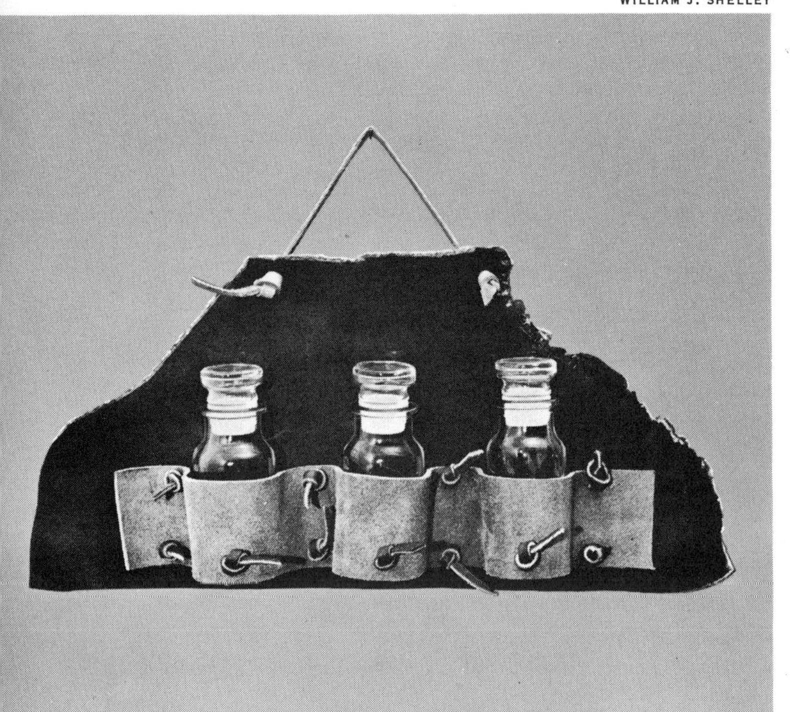

CREATE POCKETS by lacing a strip of leather to backing. Jars rest on pieces of lace knotted through bottom edge of strip.

STEVE SMITH

WALL SECRETARY can be made to any size you like, with as many pockets as you need. Hang it from loops riveted to top.

Leather-covered Objects

Besides making things entirely out of leather, you'll probably want to cover the surfaces of articles with leather. Innumerable items—including desk accessories, notebook holders, and frames of all types—are popular.

Most often, the leather can just be cemented to the surface of an object with contact or rubber cement. A rounded surface can be more difficult to cover, so you might start with articles having a flat surface. Try fitting paper or felt over the surface first.

WILLIAM J. SHELLEY

WHETHER YOU CEMENT scraps randomly onto the surface (left bottle) or fit them precisely (right bottle), try wrapping paper or felt around the bottle first, to make a pattern that will provide an idea of how the pieces will fit.

WILLIAM J. SHELLEY

A PLAIN WOODEN BOX is attractive when covered with leather. On this one, different colored scraps were first fitted over the surface and then cemented down. Corners and sides were done separately, the leather was not folded over them.

CEMENTING is a common method of securing leather to a surface, but you might like to try others. The rectangles on the wastebasket below were threaded onto thongs and slipped over basket, then the ends of the thongs were tied together tightly.

WILLIAM J. SHELLEY

OBJECTS that have corners or curved surfaces can be difficult to cover, and so you might want to start with articles having flat surfaces only. A mirror frame such as the one shown here is only one of the possibilities.

WILLIAM J. SHELLEY

Leather Jewelry

Bracelets, necklaces, pendants, choker collars, hair barrettes, and even earrings and cuff links can be made easily out of leather scraps.

A hair barrette is perhaps the simplest piece of jewelry to create. It is just a piece of leather cut into an interesting shape with holes punched for a short wooden dowel to go through. Leather dye or paint and stamped, tooled, or burned designs add a decorative flair.

The possibilities for bracelets, necklaces, and choker collars are many. You can thread pieces of leather onto thongs, cut a strip of leather and braid it, or try macrameing thongs. To fasten the ends of the leather, use a snap, short lengths of thong, or even a buckle.

Cuff links can be made by knotting the ends of short pieces of thin lace through small pieces of leather. Design a set of earrings that hang from screw-back or clipped earring fixtures, available at craft and jewelry shops. Pendants can be made by hanging a piece of leather from a length of thong.

WILLIAM J. SHELLEY

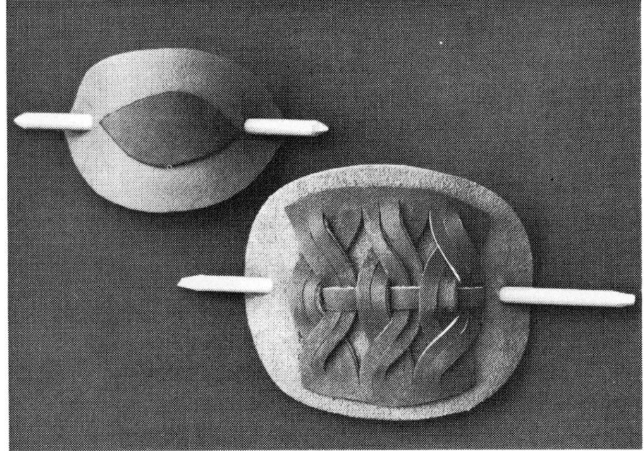

HAIR BARRETTE is just a piece of thick leather with holes for a length of dowel. Cut the leather to any shape you like.

WILLIAM J. SHELLEY

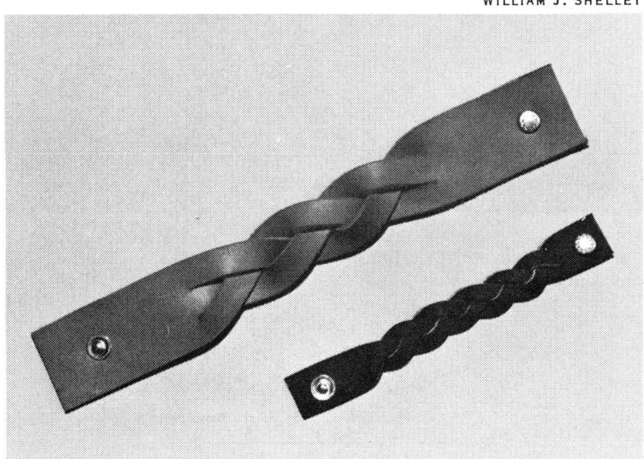

CHOKER NECKLACES and bracelets are similar. Fasten ends with a thong or snap. See page 38 for braiding instructions.

WILLIAM J. SHELLEY

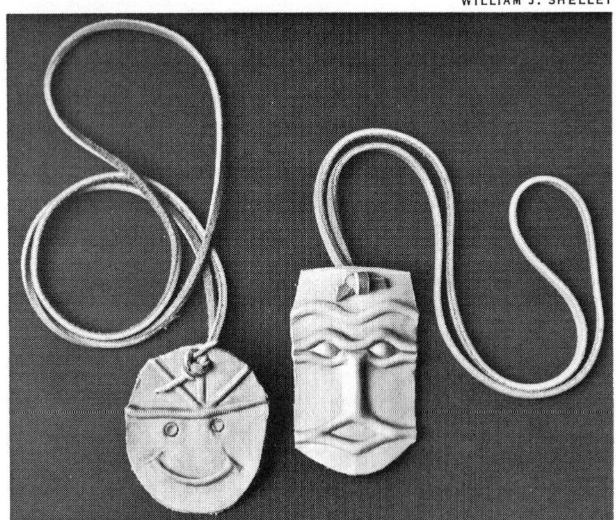

PENDANTS can be molded leather (page 79) or just a piece that has been interestingly cut, dyed, and decorated.

WILLIAM J. SHELLEY

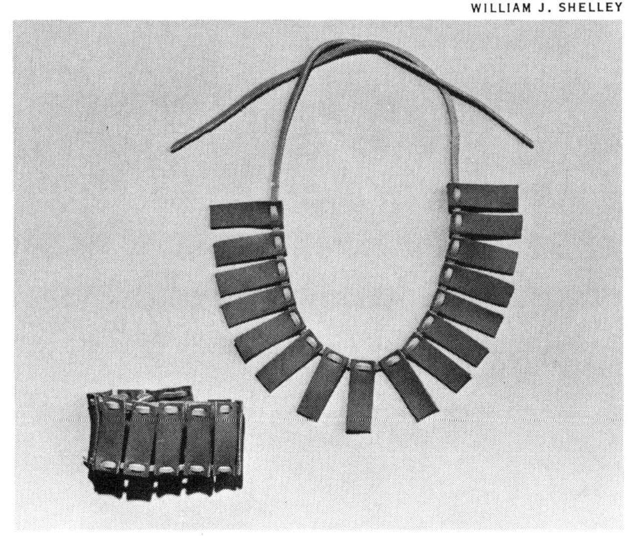

NECKLACE was made by threading rectangles cut from pieces of 6 ounce scraps onto a thong. Try different colored leather.

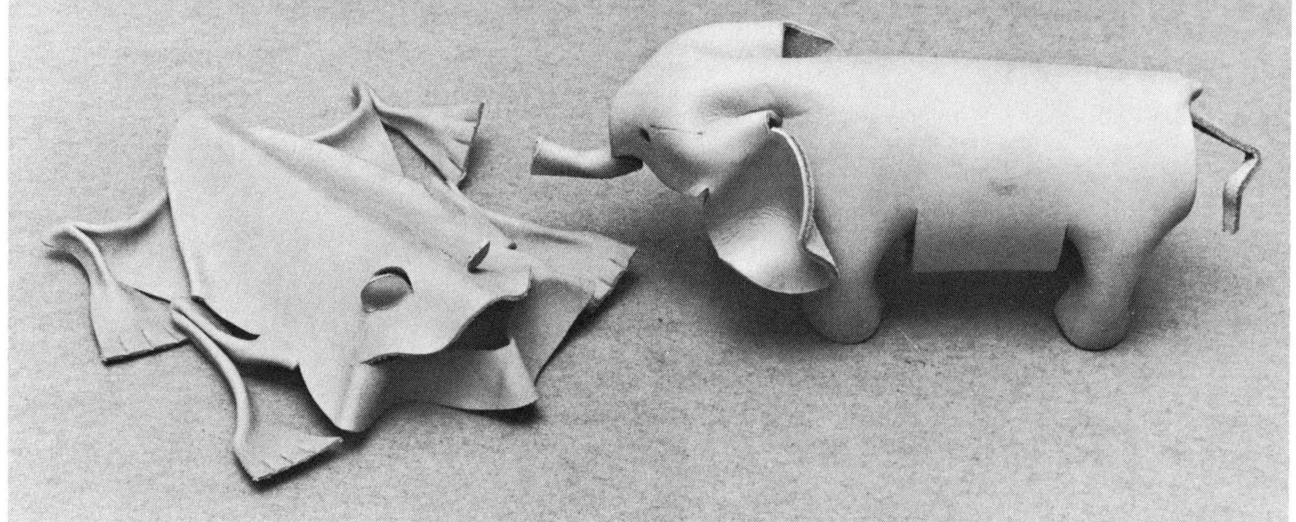

WILLIAM J. SHELLEY

MOLDED LEATHER ANIMALS start as a flat piece of leather cut to the outline of the animal desired. In the fashion of kiragami paper cutting, slits are made for the eyes and mouth and so that the body can be rounded.

Molded Leather Forms

WILLIAM J. SHELLEY

MOLDED BAS-RELIEF is laminated to this leather cup, created by cementing a piece of leather into a cylinder.

An interesting technique that you might enjoy is molding leather. It involves dampening a piece of leather, bending and shaping it to the form you want, and then allowing it to dry. Choose 1-2 ounce oak-tanned cowhide or "rawhide" leather.

There are several ways of molding leather. The easiest is to bend the dampened leather into the shape you want with your hands. Another is to stretch the leather over a form until it has dried. The form you use might be anything from a carved piece of wood to egg beater blades.

WILLIAM J. SHELLEY

WALL PLAQUE is created by dampening the leather, pinching up the raised facial features, then allowing the leather to dry.

WILLIAM J. SHELLEY

A LEATHER MOSAIC wall hanging is a fun decoration for a child's room. This one is made entirely of scrap leather available at most leather shops. Try using different kinds, thicknesses, and colors of leather.

Art with Leather

WILLIAM J. SHELLEY

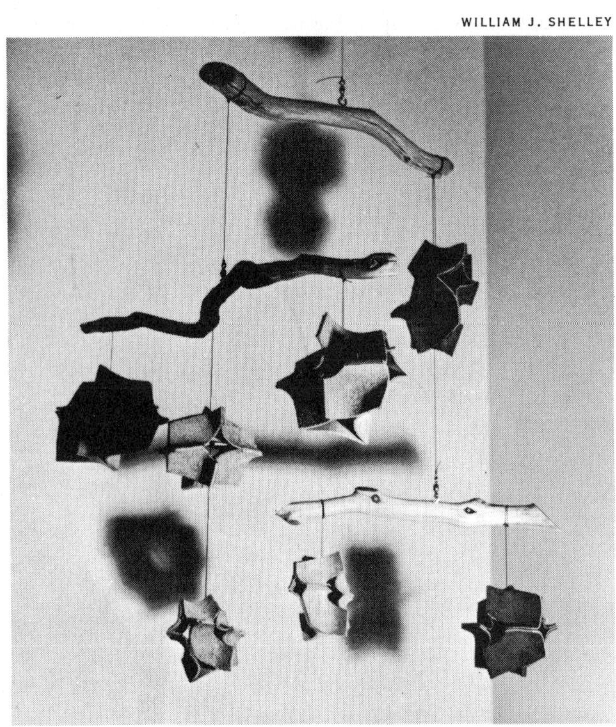

PIECES OF LEATHER cemented into geometric shapes and driftwood complement each other in this simple mobile.

Why not use leather in a purely decorative manner? A mosaic made from different kinds and colors of scrap leather can enliven a wall or cover a table top. On your next trip to the library, check out a book on kiragami paper cutting or origami paper folding and see if any of the ideas can be adapted to leather. (The leather basket on page 35 was made using kirigami techniques.) Collage is another leather possibility, and a bagful of scrap leather (available at craft and leather shops) will provide plenty of material. By molding, lacing, sewing, riveting, snapping, and cementing pieces of leather, a pleasing sculpture or an abstract form can be created.

Designed for a child's room, the wall hanging shown above was created by cementing leather forms onto a plywood base covered with burlap. Try cementing only the edges of the shapes (arms, legs, head) to the board to give them a three-dimensional effect.

The mobile (left) was made from pieces of leather cemented together into cube shapes. For ideas on shapes and forms to use for a similar mobile, look through books on paper folding or read the craft section of a family magazine or newspaper supplement.